JOHN BOYES
KING OF THE WA-KIKUYU

Library of African Adventure
Mike Resnick, series editor

African Nature Notes and Reminiscences
by Frederick Courteney Selous
King of the Wa-Kikuyu by John Boyes
*Elephant Hunting in East Equatorial Africa
by Arthur H. Neumann

*forthcoming

JOHN BOYES

KING OF THE WA-KIKUYU

A TRUE STORY OF TRAVEL AND ADVENTURE IN AFRICA

WRITTEN BY HIMSELF

EDITED BY

G. W. L. BULPETT

INTRODUCTION BY

MIKE RESNICK, SERIES EDITOR

THE LIBRARY OF AFRICAN ADVENTURE

St. Martin's Press
New York

Library of Congress Cataloging-in-Publication Data

Boyes, John.
King of the Wa-Kikuyu / John Boyes.
    p.   cm. — (The Library of African adventure)
Originally published: London : Methuen, 1911.
ISBN 0-312-09320-9
1. Boyes, John, 1874–1951.   2. Explorers—Kenya—
Biography.   3. Kikuyu (African people)—Social life and
customs.   4. Kenya—Description and travel.   I. Title.
II. Series.
DT433.545.K55B69   1993
967.62'03'092—dc20   93-14837   CIP

First Edition: June 1993
10 9 8 7 6 5 4 3 2 1

TO

WILLIAM NORTHROP McMILLAN

IN MEMORY OF MANY

TRAMPS TOGETHER

INTRODUCTION TO THIS FACSIMILE EDITION

THERE have been a number of great hunters in the annals of African history.

There have been some equally brilliant explorers.

But when it comes to the category of Opportunist, one name stands out from all the others: hunter, explorer, farmer, trader, ivory poacher, gambler, reprobate, soldier, sailor, and yes, even king, the one and only John Boyes.

John had a humble enough beginning—and a humble enough ending, too. He was born in Yorkshire in 1874, the son of a shoemaker, and he died in Nairobi in 1951, spending his final days running a dairy farm and driving his own milkwagon. But John Boyes put more living, more scheming, more out-and-out *adventure* into his seventy-seven years than any half-dozen men combined.

His life—his *real* life—began when he was fourteen. He had no intention of following in his father's footsteps, and he hopped a ship bound for distant ports, prepared for a life at sea. It almost turned out to be a very brief life *in* sea, as the young cabin boy was washed overboard during a storm in the North Sea and barely made it back aboard. He got to see quite a bit of the world during the next decade, not always in the happiest of circumstances: He was marooned off Rotterdam, hospitalized with yellow fever on the Amazon, and stricken with malaria while navigating the rivers of West Africa.

All of his experiences to this point—including having his ship rammed in the middle of the night—simply whetted his appetite for more exotic adventure. While his ship was docked in Durban, South Africa, he heard of the Second Matabele War, which was taking place in Southern Rhodesia, so he jumped ship and set off, on foot, for Bulawayo, which was close to a thousand miles away.

Once there—and it was no easy task *getting* there—he joined the Matabeleland Mounted Police, couldn't find enough action to suit him, and soon transferred to the Afrikander Corps, which boasted such officers as F. C. Selous and R. S. S. Baden-Powell, who later founded the Boy Scouts. A severe spell of dysentery didn't stop John from enjoying the war—if he ever willingly avoided a battle during his life, it has gone unrecorded—and when it was over he returned to Bulawayo, where he founded the Colonial Fruit and Produce Stores of Bulawayo, a business that eventually made over one hundred thousand pounds, but not until long after the restless Boyes had sold out to his partner, a man named Frielich.

A brief stint as a Shakespearean actor in Durban was followed by a trip up the east coast of the continent until he wound up in Mombasa in 1898 and began creating his legend in earnest.

It was at this time that the Mombasa-Uganda Railway—known as the "Lunatic Line," for, as was argued in the British Parliament, only a lunatic would spend a thousand pounds a mile to build the damned thing—was under construction. When the railway reached Tsavo, the two most famous man-eating lions in history brought work to a halt by dining almost nightly on the imported coolie laborers until Lieutenant Colonel J. H. Patterson finally dispatched them. But in truth, the railway had more serious, if not more newsworthy, problems facing it. There was disease, there was drought, there were hostile tribes, there were mass defections, and there was the enormous task of supplying food for 25,000 coolies.

Now, John didn't know anything about railroads or coolies when he reached Mombasa. But he did know that the Sudanese Mutiny had broken out in Uganda, and the army was offering top dollar to anyone who could transport food from the coast to Lake Victoria. John figured it was easy money, bought a caravan of donkeys, loaded them down with boxes of food, hired some donkey drivers, and headed west. After a month the last donkey had died from the bite of the tsetse fly, so John loaded the boxes onto the backs of his donkey drivers. A couple of days later he came down with another attack of malaria, and when the fever broke and he came to his senses, he found himself surrounded by hundreds of boxes, a bunch of dead donkeys, and no drivers. They had all deserted.

John was nothing if not self-confident. He concluded that if this could happen to such a competent man as himself, it had probably happened to everyone who had gone ahead of him as well, so he simply made camp and waited—and sure enough, before long a number of porters who had deserted other caravans came down the trail on their way back to Mombasa, and John, gun in hand, simply explained the facts of life to them and enlisted them, somewhat less than voluntarily, into his service.

He finally delivered the food and was paid two hundred pounds for his efforts—enough for a man to live like a king for a decade in East Africa. But John, never satisfied and always looking for an angle, decided that if he could make money supplying the soldiers in Uganda, he could make even easier money supplying people who were not quite so far away.

Which was when he discovered the railroad, and its crying need for food.

Now, John knew that *he* couldn't single-handedly supply food to 25,000 coolies no matter how many gazelles and elands he shot. But the notion of all that potential profit got him to thinking, which was always what he did best, and he cast about for some means by which he could supply the railroad with all food it required. So he looked at a map, and found that there was a huge area to the north known as Kikuyuland, which was closed to whites. He did a little research and discovered that Kikuyuland housed the most fertile farmland in all of Kenya. (In fact, this land later became the "White Highlands," one of the major causes of conflict in the Mau Mau Emergency.)

John walked north to the border of Kikuyuland, hired some locals who knew the Kikuyu dialect, and prepared to enter the forbidden country, when the British refused to let him pass. Undeterred, John led his crew around the perimeter to a less-developed district, a journey of well over a month, and crossed over the border from there.

Although a number of huge caravans hoping to set up trade with the Kikuyu had been slaughtered, it never occurred to John that he might be biting off more than he could chew. After three days he came to a Kikuyu village, ruled by a chief named Karuri, and faced down a war party of 500, demanding an audience with their leader.

Karuri had never seen a white man before, and was so

fascinated by John's appearance that he put off killing him long enough for John to lie about all the firepower that would be brought to bear on the village if anything untoward should befall him. Karuri pointed out that John had only one gun, but John replied that it was a magical rifle that could shoot through six men at once—and to prove it, he loaded a solid cartridge into it and fired it at a nearby baobab tree (which is known for its soft, pulpy wood). He told Karuri to examine the tree, and he would see that the bullet came out the other side—and furthermore, added John, far from stopping, it had gone through still more trees off in the distance. The bluff worked, he and Karuri exchanged gifts, and Karuri even built him a hut in the village.

The very next morning, John was awakened by savage war cries: The village was being attacked by a rival Kikuyu band. He raced out of his hut, rifle in hand, opened fire on the attackers, and killed a number of them while the rest fled in terror. He than explained to Karuri that the men were bound to come back in greater force, and the only things standing between the village and its destruction were John and his weapon. Karuri was enough of a realist to agree, and insisted that John remain there, though he still refused to trade with him.

But the best of John's miracles was yet to come. After the battle was over, he went among the injured men, most of whom could be expected to lose an arm or leg to gangrene as infection set in, and treated them with iodoform, the first disinfectant the Kikuyu had ever seen. When the warriors began recovering from their wounds, Karuri finally found something worth trading for, and John, exchanging an amount of iodoform equal to that of a man's thumbnail for every twenty pounds of flour, was soon in business. He sold the flour to the railroad for four hundred pounds, then gathered up more porters and returned to Kikuyuland.

While back at Karuri's village, John heard of another village that had attacked and slaughtered an Arab caravan that was said to have possessed more than one hundred rifles. He quickly organized an army and conquered the village, and while he found only thirty rifles to be in working order—the Kikuyu hadn't known what they were, and had simply thrown them in a huge heap—he now had a blooded army plus the only thirty-one firearms in Kikuyuland.

One by one the other tribes asked to join with him. There was opposition as well, but after one final battle, in which he came as close as he ever had to losing his life, John emerged triumphant and became the acknowledged King of the Kikuyu. The entire ascent from intruder to monarch took just over a year.

John learned to speak Kikuyu, but when dealing with new tribes he fell back upon an old native ruse of pretending he could not understand the language, which often gave him an advantage. He created a network of wandering minstrels who gathered news from his entire kingdom and brought it straight back to his waiting ears. At one point he bought Kirinyaga—now known as Mount Kenya—for the sum of four goats, extending his dominion appreciably. His greatest regret was not shooting a native who showed signs of smallpox; instead he had the man confined to a cabin until he could import some medication, but the guard released him a few days later, he wandered to another village, and soon an epidemic ensued.

By this time, John was so preoccupied with his duties as king that his business of supplying food had dwindled away to nothing, so when some British soldiers showed up and announced that the Crown was taking control of

Kikuyuland, he was overjoyed.

His happiness was short-lived. Very soon afterward a troop of ten native soldiers entered his village and, under British orders, placed him under arrest for the crime of *dacoity*, which was loosely described as "banditry" (though his greatest sin seems to have been flying the Union Jack without official permission), and told him that he would have to stand trial in Nairobi. As they marched him through Kikuyuland, thousands of his loyal subjects, done up in war paint and brandishing their spears, joined the caravan to accompany their king. Eventually the soldiers washed their hands of the matter and made John march a few miles ahead of them and tell his people not to molest them. Once he left Kikuyuland, he was accompanied the rest of the way to Nairobi by 200 of his personal bodyguard, while the ten native troops followed very discreetly in his wake.

The trial was eventually held in Mombasa, and was promptly thrown out of court, the judge ruling that Boyes had done the best he could for Britain under trying circumstances.

John took some time off to buy a farm, explore the White Nile, and write his first set of memoirs, *John Boyes, King of the Wa-Kikuyu*, which you are holding in your hands, and then began looking for money and adventure again. Opportunity soon beckoned to him from the Lado Enclave.

The Enclave was a piece of land that had formerly been part of the Belgian Congo bordering on Uganda, but due to intricate diplomatic maneuverings it had literally become a no-man's-land upon the death of King Leopold of Belgium in 1909. It also happened to hold the greatest concentration of elephants left in Africa.

All the great elephant hunters of the day made a beeline to the Enclave upon news of Leopold's death. There was Karamojo Bell, and Deaf Banks, and Mickey Norton, and Charlie Ross, and Billy Pickering, and Bill Buckley—and of course there was John Boyes.

John wasn't much of a hunter, and he wasn't much of a tracker, but he was one hell of a thinker, and while Bell and the others used their bushcraft to find the fabled herds, John chose an especially Boyesian method: He entered Belgian territory, represented himself as a trader, and made friends with the Belgian district commissioner. After an appropriate number of drinks, he let it slip that he was terrified of elephants, and was going to be trading in the Lado Enclave—and the commissioner, as a gesture of friendship, gave John a map with all the herds marked on it so he would know which areas to avoid! Within a month, John had collected thirteen thousand dollars' worth of ivory.

Then there was the time that John was crossing the savage Abyssinian desert with a string of donkeys and horses he had agreed to purchase and bring back for the British troops stationed in Nairobi. Along the way, a local district commissioner asked him to load some ivory he had confiscated from poachers onto the mules and deliver it to the Governor. It was a long, arduous journey, fraught with danger, and John demanded a very high price, which the commissioner agreed to—but when he arrived in Nairobi the Governor refused to honor the agreement and paid him a lesser amount.

Some men would have raised hell and got themselves thrown in jail. Some would have shrugged and accepted their losses. Not John.

He wandered over to the bar of the Norfolk Hotel, trying to figure out how to get his money, and found himself in the middle of a meeting of sisal growers who were enraged by some new government regulation. John promptly took control of the meeting, and within a few minutes was leading a march on the Governor's home. Once there, he told the furious farmers to wait outside, that he would speak to the Governor.

Upon gaining entrance to the Governor's house, he took that poor official by the arm, led him to the window, and explained that these outraged citizens standing out there in the street were ready to lynch him for shortchanging poor John Boyes. The Governor gave John the rest of the money due him, and John went outside and told the farmers that the Governor was looking into their problem and to go home peacefully. The next morning, his bank account once again healthy, he was off in search of more adventure.

John turns up in the oddest places in the history of East Africa. Though an uneducated Yorkshireman, he was a friend of Karen Blixen (Isak Dinesen) and even played host to Theodore Roosevelt while poaching ivory in the Lado Enclave. In fact, at one point during Roosevelt's visit, John offered to put a force of ivory poachers at the American's disposal if Roosevelt would remain in Africa and devote himself to opening up the Congo for commercial exploitation.

"He was," recalled Boyes in his second memoir, *Company of Adventurers*, "deeply moved by this offer; and long afterwards he told a friend that no honor ever paid him had impressed and tempted him like that which he received from the poachers of the Lado Enclave."

John also appears in the diary of Fred Roy, a trader: "*August 28, 1907*: John Boyes, who was up in Golbo to relieve Zaphiro, had a very narrow escape. While riding his mule he was seized round the waist by an elephant and thrown to the ground. Not being stunned, he proceeded to get up. The elephant grabbed him again, this time throwing him in the air, and with presence of mind Boyes caught hold of a tree. The elephant, not seeing him, looked round and, finding a boulder which he mistook for a man, sat down and rubbed away until scared off."

A young John Alfred Jordan, himself a notorious ivory poacher, was impressed enough by the sight of Boyes riding through Nairobi on his Abyssinian mule that he remembered it half a century later, when writing his own memoirs.

At various times during his life John also ran the Norfolk stores, worked as a white hunter, was a gambler, and, though no longer a young man, rose to the rank of lieutentant colonel of the Legion of Frontiersmen after fighting the Germans in East Africa during World War I.

I personally find him the most fascinating and multifaceted of all Kenyan pioneers, and have made fictional use of him as "Catamount Greene" in *Paradise* (Tor, 1989) and as himself as Theodore Roosevelt's companion in my award-nominated novella *Bully* (Axolotl Press, 1990; Tor Double, 1991). I also appropriated a number of his schemes and scams in my African parody, *Adventures* (New American Library, 1985).

He was a little man, small and wiry, but he left a big footprint across the pages of East African history. He is perhaps best captured by Lord Cranworth, who described him thus:

"Although of amazingly strong and resilient constitution, there was nothing outstandingly impressive in his appearance or physique. The country wherein he operated was the wildest and least explored, and the tribes he encountered were the most savage and barbarous. I

INTRODUCTION

would judge that he had less support, near and distant,
moral or actual, than any of his kindred rovers."

Fortunately, support was one thing John Boyes never
needed.

—Mike Resnick

JOHN BOYES
KING OF THE WA-KIKUYU

EDITOR'S PREFACE

THE following pages describe a life of adventure in the more remote parts of Africa—adventures such as the explorer and sportsmen do not generally encounter. The man to whom the episodes narrated in this book refer has been personally known to me for ten years. We have hunted big game and explored together many a time in the African jungle; and as it is principally at my instigation that he has put the following account of his experiences into writing, I think it is due to him and to the public that I should make known my responsibility in the matter.

It seemed to me that the adventures John Boyes underwent were something quite out of the common; in these matter-of-fact days they may be said to be almost unique. In the days of exploration and discovery, when Captain Cook and such heroes lived and thrived, they were perhaps common enough; but every year the opportunities of such adventure get more and more remote, and as the uttermost parts of the earth are brought under the influence of civilization will become ever more impossible. For this reason alone a story such as told here seems to be worth recording.

7

There is no attempt at literary style.   The man tells his tale in a simple, matter-of-fact way, and, as his Editor, I have thought it better from every point of view to leave his words as he has written them.

The reader will judge for himself as to the interest of the adventures here related, but I think any one will admit that no ordinary force of character was necessary to carry them through to a successful issue.   The whole life of the author during the time he was a wanderer in the Kikuyu country, and later while he was practically supreme ruler of the tribe—a tribe numbering half a million of people—was one of imminent daily risk.

Each hour he went about with his life in his hands, and if he came out scatheless from the mêlée, he has only to thank his courage, nerve, and resource.   All these qualities he obviously possessed in a high degree.

He appears to have been harshly treated by the British East Africa authorities.   Doubtless much that he did was grossly misrepresented to them by more or less interested parties.   He certainly did yeoman's service to the colony in its early days by opening up an unknown and hostile country which lay right on the borderland of the Uganda Railway, at that time in course of construction.   His energetic action enabled the coolies on the line to work safe from many hostile attacks.   He supplied them with the food without which they would have starved—all for a very small reward, and at great personal risk to himself.   But the love of adventure was in him, and such people do not work for profit alone.   The life itself brings its own reward.

An impartial observer will perhaps be able to under-stand the point of view of the British Administration, and will appreciate their difficulty, indeed their ability, to allow an independent white power to rule beside their own; but the public will judge for themselves whether they set about to do what they did with regard to John Boyes in the most tactful way, or whether they treated a brave fellow-countryman in the manner he deserved.

                                    C. W. L. B.

August, 1911.

CONTENTS

JOHN BOYES, KING OF THE WA-KIKUYU

CHAPTER I

Early youth—I run away to sea on a fishing-boat—
Hardships of the life—Take service on a tugboat—
Life on board a tramp—First view of tropical African
coast—A collision at sea—Land at Durban, 1895

THIS book is simply an attempt to set down, in a
plain and straightforward manner, some account
of the various experiences and adventures of the
author during a period of some fifteen years spent in
hunting, trading, and exploring, principally on the
eastern side of the African continent. The title has
been suggested by some episodes in the narrative, the
main facts of which are within the recollection of
many of the white men now in British East Africa.
These episodes caused somewhat of a stir at the time,
and the author had to stand his trial before the local
courts on a capital charge as a direct consequence of
the facts here narrated.

I was born at Hull, in the East Riding of Yorkshire, on 11 May, 1874, so that at the time of writing
this book I am still a comparatively young man. I
lived there with my parents until I was six years of
age, when I was sent to Germany to be educated at
the little town of Engelfingen, where my parents had
some relatives living, and it was here that I received
all the schooling I have ever had. This early educa-

tion has left its mark on me, and even at the present day I sometimes find it difficult to express myself correctly in English—a fact, I hope, an indulgent public will take into consideration.

At the age of thirteen my schooling in Germany ended, and I returned home to my parents, who wished me to continue my schooldays in Hull, as I had received no English education whatever; but I strongly objected to going to school again, and, evading their efforts to control me, spent most of my time about the docks, watching the vessels in and out.

By this time my mind was bent on a seafaring life, and I lost no opportunity of scraping acquaintance with sailors from the different ships, whose tales of the various countries they had visited and the strange sights they had seen fired my imagination and made me more determined than ever to follow the sea.

I practically lived on the docks, and one of my greatest delights was to pilot a boat round them, or to get some of my many friends among the sailors to allow me to help with odd jobs about a vessel, such as cleaning up the decks or polishing the brasswork; and I was fully determined to get away to sea at the first opportunity.

My keenest desire, at this time, was to enter the Navy, but my parents would not hear of my going to sea, and without their consent I could not be accepted, so that idea had to be abandoned. I was determined to be a sailor, however, and kept my eyes open for a chance of getting away on one of the fishing-vessels sailing out of Hull, among which were still many of the old sailing-boats, which have now been almost entirely displaced by the steam-trawlers. When I had been at home about six months the longed-for chance came. I got to know that one of the trawlers was to sail at a very early hour one morning, so, stealing out of the house before any of the other members of the family were about, I made my way down to the docks. This being before the days of the large tonnage steam-trawlers, the vessels carried only about five hands, and finding that the boat on which I had set my mind was in need of a cook and cabin-boy, I offered my services, and was duly signed on. My knowledge of the work was nil, but, to my surprise and delight, the captain asked no awkward questions, and I found myself enrolled as a member of the crew of my first ship, which was bound for the North Sea fishing-grounds, and was expected to be away for about three months.

I was very seasick on this first voyage—the only time in my life that I have ever suffered from that complaint—and the life proved less attractive than I had expected. In those days the lads on the fishing-boats were very badly treated, and though I had not so much to complain of in this respect, I found it a very trying life at the best. The work itself was very hard, and I was liable to be called up at any hour of the day or night to prepare hot coffee or do anything that any member of the crew wanted me to do.

It was on this voyage that I had a very narrow escape of being drowned in a gale which we encountered. We had taken in the second reef of the main-sail, which hung over like a huge hammock, and I was ordered aloft to perform the operation known as reefing the lacing. As I was crawling along the sail a heavy sea struck the ship, carrying the boom over to the weather side, which caused the sail to flap over and pitch me head first into the sea. Fortunately for me, the accident was witnessed by the crew, one of whom seized a boathook, and, as I came within reach, managed to catch me by the belt, and so succeeded in hauling me on board again, feeling very miserable and, of course, drenched to the skin, but otherwise none the worse for my adventure.

With this exception, there was little out of the ordinary in my life on the trawler, unless I mention an experience I had when we were lying off the then British island of Heligoland.

It was the custom for the captains of the various boats to go ashore all together, in one boat, on Sundays, and the crew also often took advantage of the opportunity of a run ashore. One Sunday they had all gone ashore, leaving me in sole charge of the ship, my principal duties being to prepare the dinner and stoke the boiler of the donkey-engine so as to keep steam up ready for hauling up the anchor at a moment's notice. Soon after they had gone some lads came off in a shore-boat, and as I could speak German we were soon on the best of terms, and of course I had to give them biscuits and show them round the ship. So engrossed was I with my new-found friends that I forgot all about the boiler, until I noticed a strong smell of burning. We all raced to the engine-room, to find that the boiler was red hot and had set fire to the woodwork round it. Not knowing what else to do, we chopped away the woodwork and threw it overboard, and so prevented the fire spreading. Scenting trouble ahead, my friends took to their boat and cleared out, while I decided that it would be wise to disappear for a time also, and so hid myself in a part of the ship where I thought I was least likely to be found. The captain made a big fuss when he discovered the damage, and I heard him calling loudly for me, but I thought it would be wise to remain out of sight until he had had time to cool down; so I stayed where I was, turning up again next morning. He did not say much when I appeared, probably because he thought awkward questions might be asked if any bother was made as to why a youngster like myself had been left in sole charge of the vessel.

I returned to Hull after six months with the fishing fleet, fairly sick of life on a trawler, and with my mind made up to try for something better in the seafaring line.

My great idea was to get abroad and see something of the world, and I should, so I thought, stand a better chance of doing this if I went to Liverpool and tried to get a ship there. Having no money—my entire worldly possessions consisted, at this time, of a few spare clothes—I set out to walk the whole distance from Hull.

For a lad of fifteen this was no light undertaking, but, as in other instances in my career, the very difficulties only seemed to make the idea more attractive; so I started boldly off. Having no very clear idea of the route to be followed, I made for York, and then continued my journey by way of Leeds and Manchester. I had no money, so, to procure the little food I could allow myself, I pawned my spare clothes at different places on my way, and helped out my scanty meals with an occasional raw turnip or carrot; and though I had to go on rather short commons towards the end of my journey, I managed to get through without being reduced to begging. Of course I had nothing to spare for lodgings, and used to sleep out during the day, continuing my journey at night, and as it was early in the year—about the beginning of May—I found the cold at times bitter, but this was my greatest hardship.

After a rather weary journey I eventually arrived in Liverpool, very footsore but in good spirits, and finding a lodging-house in the seamen's quarter of the town kept by an old sailor who was willing to take me in on trust until I got a ship, I took up my quarters there, agreeing to repay him as soon as I got a berth.

I still had a strong inclination for the Navy, so I applied at the recruiting office, but, as I could not show my parents' consent, they refused to accept me, and I had to look elsewhere. At last I got a berth on a tugboat, called the *Knight of St. John*, which was going out to Rotterdam to tow a barque, the *Newman Hall*, into Liverpool.

While at Rotterdam I managed to get into another scrape, but, fortunately, it was not a very serious one, though I suffered some discomfort. It was known on board that I could speak German well, so I was sent ashore to buy cigars and tobacco for the officers and crew. I must have been longer away than they expected, as when I got back to the quay the boat was gone. Having no money left, I was in a fix for a night's lodging, until I noticed a small wooden hut on the beach, apparently unoccupied, so, taking shelter in this, I made myself as comfortable as possible and went to sleep. On waking the next morning I was astonished to find the shanty surrounded by water. It turned out to be a hut built for the use of bathers, and at high tide was always surrounded by the sea; consequently I had to stay where I was and wait more or less patiently until the tide went down far enough to enable me to wade ashore. While I was wondering what to do next I saw the tug coming along close inshore, and shouting until I attracted attention, I was soon aboard again.

Having got our tow-line aboard the barque, we started on our return journey to Liverpool, but had scarcely got clear of land before it commenced to blow heavily, and the sea became so rough that we had to part company with the barque, which, fortunately, drifted back to Rotterdam, while we found ourselves with only sufficient coal to take us into Dover.

I did not stop long with the tug, as I came to the conclusion that there was little chance of getting on in my profession if I was content to simply knock about from ship to ship. If I was ever to get an officer's certificate, I must start by getting a berth as A.B. (able seaman), in an ocean-going ship, so that I could put in the four years' regular sea service which I should have to show before going up for my certificate, of which at least twelve months had to be on a sailing ship trading to foreign ports. I therefore looked out for a suitable berth, and at last shipped on a barque, the *Lake Simcoe*, trading to South America.

I had, as usual, my shade of incident during the voyage.

Whilst trading in Brazil, we made a trip up the River Amazon, during which I got a touch of yellow fever, and on arriving at Laguña, where we had to take some logwood on board, I was put ashore to go into hospital. I do not know what alterations have been made since I was there, but at that time the hospital was a gloomy enough building, with heavily barred slits in the wall for windows, and used indifferently as hospital, lunatic asylum, and gaol, while the strong resemblance to a prison was heightened by the fact that the place was always guarded by a detachment of soldiers.

The hospital arrangements were disgusting and reckless, no regard being paid either to sanitation or the prevention of infection. All manner of diseases were mixed indiscriminately in the same ward, while the duties of orderlies and attendants on the patients were undertaken by some of the more harmless among the lunacy cases!

One gruesome discovery which I made soon after my entry was that the establishment possessed only one coffin, which had to do duty for each fatal case in turn, being made with a sliding bottom, which reduced the work of lowering the corpse into the grave to a minimum. When a case ended fatally, the corpse was placed in this coffin—which was always kept in the ward—and taken out for burial, the coffin being afterwards returned to its place in the hospital, in full view of the other patients! As there were generally three or four funerals every day, it may be easily imagined that the effect on those left behind was not the most cheering.

One other custom in the hospital struck me as very peculiar. When a patient became very bad the attendant generally gave him a spoonful of a substance which, from the smell, I have since thought must have been opium. Whether or not this was merely given to relieve pain I cannot say : I only know that the patient invariably died soon after taking it.

One day the spoon was brought to me, so I asked the attendant, one of the harmless lunatics, to place it on the table by my bedside. Occupying the adjoining pallet was a Brazilian soldier, who, waking up in the night, asked if he might have the stuff in the spoon, as he was in terrible pain. Thinking it might relieve him, I made no objection, and he eagerly swallowed the lot. The next morning he was dead!

After this experience, I was anxious to get out of my present quarters as rapidly as possible, and a chance came a day or two afterwards of which I at once took advantage. It happened to be Sunday, and my bed being close to one of the slits which served for windows, I heard the voices of some of the crew of the *Lake Simcoe* outside. I at once shouted to attract their attention, and begged them to get me out of this awful hole. Recognising my voice, they threw themselves on the soldiers guarding the place, and, after a struggle, managed to get in, and carried me off. I was fearfully weak, and scarcely able to stand, but they managed to get me aboard ship at last, where, with proper attention, I soon recovered.

On the homeward voyage we had terribly rough weather in the Atlantic, and the ship became top-heavy, listing to such an extent that the fore-yard-arms were practically in the water the whole time. For days we were drenched to the skin with the big seas which broke over the vessel continually, and the hull being practically under water, I wrapped myself in a blanket—having no dry clothing left—and kept my watch seated on the mast, which dipped in and out of the water with every roll of the ship.

To add to our misfortune, scurvy broke out very badly among the crew, owing to the wretched quality of the food, and, altogether, we were very thankful when we at last made Falmouth harbour.

Shortly after my return I joined the Royal Naval

Reserve, in which I had to put in a month's drill every year, as I was still bent on getting into the Navy, if possible, and I thought that, if I could work my way up to a Lieutenancy in the Reserve, I might manage it that way.

By this time I had done my twelve months in a sailing ship; so, by shipping on steamers trading to different parts, I was able to visit many interesting places. For twelve months I was on a boat trading between the various ports on the coast of India, and on another voyage was in a ship taking pilgrims from Port Said to Jedda. Our passengers on this voyage were chiefly Arabs and Turks on their way to Mecca. For another trip I shipped in one of the Royal Niger Company's boats, and we went up the West Coast of Africa with trading goods, chiefly old flint-lock rifles and gunpowder. We also had on board two or three white men, who were going on an exploring trip into the interior.

I was very much impressed with this part of the world, the tropical scenery was so magnificent on either side of the rivers, while I was intensely interested in the natives who came down to trade with the ship. I made up my mind that I would go into the interior myself some day, and get to know more about the country and its people. As it turned out, a good many things were to happen before this intention was carried out.

During this trip I contracted malarial fever, and not being able to shake it off, had to go into hospital at Rotterdam on our return. On my recovery I spent some time on coasting vessels trading out to Guernsey, and one night, when we had put into Dungeness, through stress of weather, I had another startling experience.

Roused out of my sleep—it was my watch below—by a shout of "All hands on deck!" I rushed up, just in time to see another ship coming directly towards us. We shouted, but she kept on her course,

and in a few seconds crashed into us. Apparently
everybody lost their heads at once, and a scene of
utter confusion followed, nobody appearing to know
what to do. I saw that the yards of the two vessels
had become entangled, and expected every minute to
see them fall, and crush the boat, which was stowed
way on deck; so I made my way to the poop, and
shouted to the crew to get the boat out at once.
So great was the confusion that it is almost impossible
to say what really happened. I only know that I
eventually found myself in a boat with only one other
man, and as we pulled off we saw the ship which had
done the mischief apparently drifting away. Pulling
to her, we managed to scramble aboard, and, to our
great surprise, found that there was not a single soul
on board, and we then remembered seeing her crew
jumping on board our vessel at the time of the
collision. Everything was in apple-pie order, and the
lamp lit, and we could not find anything the matter
with the ship, so that her crew must have been seized
with a sudden fit of panic, and abandoned her in their
fright. We were on board just in time to steer her
clear of a steamer, and then we dropped anchor. The
following morning her crew returned on board, looking rather foolish, and we were transferred to our
own vessel, which was then towed to London.

I put in a claim on account of salvage, and after
a good deal of delay, found that the owners had
settled for salvage, demurrage, and loss with the
captain of the barque, who was also the owner. I
had left the ship when we reached London, but
happened to meet the captain later on in Hull, when
he invited me to accompany him to Guernsey, to see
about my share of the salvage money. At the last
minute I found that I could not go, so he promised to
write me on the matter, but on the homeward voyage
his boat was lost, and he went down with it, so the
letter never arrived. Although very disappointed at
the loss of my expected windfall, I was very glad

I had not been able to go with the captain, or I should have lost my life as well.

Since my last voyage I had been working up for my certificate, attending a Navigation School on Prince's Dock Side, in Hull : but I was doomed to disappointment, as, when I came to be medically examined, the doctor found that my eyesight was affected, and could not pass me. This was the result of the yellow fever from which I had suffered in Brazil.

After this I had to give up all hopes of the sea as a career, unless I was willing to remain before the mast all my life, and that was by no means my idea; so my thoughts turned to Africa, and I remembered the impression made on my mind by the little I had already seen of it, and the attraction which the idea of its huge unexplored districts had always had for me since my schooldays, and I decided to see what I could do out there.

Being again at the end of my money, the only way I could get there was by working my passage, and as I could not get a berth in any boat going from Hull, I went to London, and being successful, landed at Durban, in Natal, just after the Jameson Raid.

CHAPTER II

I work my way up-country to Matabeleland—
Employed as fireman on an engine—Reach Johannesburg—Trek the rest of the way to Bulawayo—Take
service in the Matabeleland Mounted Police—Join
the Africander Corps engaged in putting down the
rebellion—Go into trade in Bulawayo—Return to the
coast—I take to the stage—Work my way on an
Arab dhow to Mombasa, February, 1898—Cool
official reception

LEARNING that the Matabele War had broken
out, I made every effort to get up to the front;
but as I had had no previous experience, the military
authorities would not take me on. However, I was
determined to get to Bulawayo somehow, and with
this idea made a start by taking the train for Pieter-
maritzburg, having just enough funds left to pay the
fare. On arriving I was lucky enough to get a job
to look after the engine and boiler at a steam bakery,
and with the money I thus earned I was able to move
on, a fortnight later, to Charlestown. I had now
just enough money to pay for a night's lodging, and
the next morning I crossed the boundary between
Natal and the Transvaal, and moved on to Volksrust,
getting a glimpse of the famous Majuba Hill on my
journey.

Of course, I was open to take any job that offered,
and it so happened that I was lucky enough to get
one that very morning, as fireman on the railway.

On applying at the station, I was asked if I was
experienced in the work, and having just left a steam

bakery, and remembering my experience with the trawler's donkey engine, I modestly said that I was, and was duly engaged and told to get on the engine of the mail train for Standerton, which was standing in the station, ready to start, and get on with the work.

The driver was a Hollander who spoke very little English, which fact I looked upon as a stroke of luck, as he would be less likely to ask awkward questions. He did ask me if I had done any firing before, and I gave him the same answer as I had given to the official on the platform. He soon put me to a practical test when, looking at the gauge glass, he told me to turn on the pump to fill the boiler. I had not the slightest idea where the pump was, but, noticing that, as he gave the order he looked at a handle which was sticking out, I promptly seized that, and began working it vigorously up and down. He at once began to shout, and I found that I had made a mistake, the handle only having to be lifted to a certain point, and then a tap turned on. Seeing that the driver seemed to expect some explanation of my mistake, I remarked that the arrangement was different from those I had been used to, which was perfectly true, and this seemed to satisfy him, as he merely said that I should, no doubt, get used to it in time.

But I was fated to exhibit my ignorance still further before we started.

I was looking over the side of the engine, when the driver gave an order which I failed to understand, being engaged in watching the antics of an official on the platform, who was waving his arms and gesticulating wildly. He looked so funny that I burst out laughing, and the more I laughed the wilder he got. In the meantime the driver was grumbling, and came across to find out the cause of my laughter, and, seeing the man on the platform, turned on me, and asked why I had not reported the signal to start? It then suddenly dawned upon me that the

order that had been given me was to watch for
" Right away," but his English was so funny that
I thought he wanted me to look out for some friends
he expected.

As Standerton was two hundred miles on my way to
Bulawayo, I had thought of leaving the train there,
but my clothes had got so dirty and greasy that I
thought it best to stay on a little longer, until I had
saved enough money to get some more clothes and
help me on my way to Johannesburg.

This particular engine proved to be one of the hard-
est for firing on the whole line, and I soon found that
I had got the job because no one else would take it,
and after a fortnight on it I was so knocked up that
I decided to take a few days off, but on applying for
my pay I was told that I should have to go to Standerton to get it. This suited my book exactly, and the
idea entered my head, " Why not get a free pass to
Johannesburg? " as they had given me one to
Standerton, to draw my money. So when I drew the
money the officials at Standerton were somewhat
startled when I demanded a free pass to Johannesburg. They seemed to think I was crazy; but I
quickly assured them that I was perfectly sane and
meant to have the pass before I left the office.

They stormed and threatened, but seeing that I
did not mean to budge, they finally gave me the pass,
with the remark that the English were always so
stupid and obstinate.

Getting some fresh clothes, I boarded the train,
and at last arrived in Johannesburg. Here I found
that most of the men in the town fire brigade were
sailors, so I soon made friends, and had hopes of
getting into the brigade, but after waiting a day or
two, and seeing no prospect of an opening, I was
advised to walk round the mines to see if I could get
anything to do there, but there were plenty of others
on the same job, many of them old hands, and I
found that I stood very little chance of employment.

I was still studying how to get up to Bulawayo, which I was told would cost me about £50 by coach, then the regular means of making the journey. At one of the mines I was lucky enough to meet a sailor, and getting a warm invitation to spend a few days with him, I accepted, on the chance that something might turn up. Visiting the saloon which was the meeting-place for the miners in the evening, I became acquainted with a man named Adcock, and as a consequence of an argument on the strained relations between the Boers and Outlanders, a row arose, in which I got mixed up, and I was ordered to leave the camp. Outside I came across Adcock, who told me that he was going up to Bulawayo, and had his outfit—which consisted of twenty mule wagons and one hundred horses, which he was taking up for the Government—camped a little distance away.

This was my chance, but at first he was inclined to refuse my request to be allowed to go up with him, but on my promising to make myself as useful as possible on the journey, he finally agreed to take me. There were six white men in the party, in addition to Adcock and myself, and about fifty natives, chiefly Cape boys and Hottentots. My duties were to look after these natives and the stores.

Bulawayo was about six hundred miles up-country from Johannesburg, and the order of the march was for the white men, who were all mounted, to drive the horses in front of the caravan, while the wagons, under charge of the native drivers, followed on behind.

With a crack of his long whip like a pistol shot, each driver set his team in motion, and we started on our long trek up-country. The natives are very expert with these whips, being able, from their place at the front of the wagon, to single out any one of the ten or twelve mules which form the team before them.

My efforts as a rider were the subject of much sarcastic and good-humoured comment from my companions, but before the end of our journey I was as good a rider as any in the outfit.

The country through which we passed was for the most part open veldt, dotted with thorn-bushes, and the climate being dry and hot, the scarcity of water is a continual source of anxiety to the traveller in this part. Our animals suffered most severely, as there was no grass to be found, and after crossing the Limpopo they began to fall sick, and our progress became slower and slower with each day's march.

When we arrived at a place called Maklutsi the mules were all so utterly done up that they could go no farther, so the horses and some of the wagons went on to Salisbury, and the natives returned.

I had the choice of going back with the natives or continuing my journey on foot, and, choosing the latter course, I was provided with a small quantity of flour and some bully beef, and saying goodbye to my companions, I started out on my solitary trek.

Food at Maklutsi was very dear in consequence of the transport having been entirely disorganised by a serious outbreak of rinderpest. The price of an ordinary tin of corned beek (bully beef) had risen to 5s., and bread cost 1s. a loaf. There was no work to be got here, so I left the settlement at once and started on my 150 miles' tramp to Bulawayo.

Having no means of carrying my food comfortably, I tied up the legs of a spare pair of trousers, and putting the flour in one leg and the beef in the other, I slung these improvised provision-bags over my shoulder, along with my cooking-pots, and started off.

When I had been two days on the road I was lucky enough to fall in with a travelling companion, in the person of an old soldier named Grant, who was also making his way to Bulawayo.

We agreed to travel on together, and Grant, who

saw everything in a humorous light, enlivened the journey with his cheery conversation and good-natured chaff. He had run out of food and would have been in a tight fix if I had not come up with him; but he took everything very philosophically, and I imagine that his lively spirits would have kept him going to the last gasp.

We shared the provisions as long as they lasted, but as I had only provided for myself, the supply gradually diminished until, stopping one day for a rest near a water-hole we had found in the bush, we found that we had not a scrap of food left.

Grant had thrown himself on the ground utterly exhausted, and I went off to the pool to have a bathe. Stepping into the water, I felt something slimy under my foot, and stooping down and groping beneath my foot, I found that it was a fish of the kind known in Africa as mud-fish. They are good enough eating, and in our present famished condition promised a very appetising dish, and to my delight, on feeling round, I found that the pool was simply full of the fish, and we need have no further anxiety about food for the next few days.

I learned from the experience gained later during my journeyings through Africa that the smaller rivers all dry up after the rainy season, leaving only a few pools, such as the one we had struck, and, of course, all the fish naturally make for the deeper spots as soon as they find the water going down. This accounted for the large quantity of fish to be found in the pool, which I proceeded to catch and throw on to the bank to dry as fast as I could. Having done this, I went back to Grant to tell him of our good luck. By way of breaking the news gently, I asked him if he would like a feed of fish, to which he replied with some comical remark to the effect that he really had no appetite, thinking that I was only chaffing. However, when he found it was really true, and saw the fish I brought up to cook for our meal, he was in no way behind me in getting to work on the best meal we had had for some days.

Not wishing to waste the fish, of which we could not manage to take much with us, we stayed there for a few days and were much better for the rest. We managed to dry a little of the fish, which we took with us when we moved on again.

This proved to be the turning-point of our luck, as a few days later we were overtaken by a Boer, going up to Bulawayo with a mule-waggon, and exchanged some of our dried fish with him for a little tea, flour, and a few other things, which we had now been without for several days. He seemed a good sort, so we begged him to give us a lift, which he did willingly enough, so our troubles were over for that journey.

I was so anxious to get into Bulawayo that I left the wagon when we were still some miles from the end of our journey, and made my way ahead on foot. This was a stupid thing to do, as we were well aware that the Matabele were already out in that district. We had found all the forts, as the police posts were called, under arms on the way up. These posts, which were placed at intervals along the road, were small positions protected by earthworks and barbed-wire entanglements, and occupied by thirty or forty men, with perhaps a Maxim gun. Many of them were the scenes of desperate fights during the rising, but their very names are unknown to people in England, who only regarded the Matabele rising as one of our many little wars, and as it did not affect their every-day life, took little or no interest in it.

I was lucky enough to get safely into Bulawayo without adventure, arriving about two o'clock in the afternoon, and was not surprised to find the town under martial law. Everybody was armed, and a big laager had been formed in the market-place, where the women and children gathered when an alarm was raised.

Being directed to the office of the Matabeleland Mounted Police, I lost no time in presenting myself before the officer in charge. I found that the conditions of service were good, the pay being at the rate of 10s. a day and all found, so I was duly enrolled.

After a good bath I discarded my old clothes and reappeared in full war-paint, feeling the self-respect which accompanies the wearing of a decent suit of clothes for the first time after some months in rags.

The police had no recognised uniform, but all wore a khaki suit, with a slouch hat, the different troops being known by the colour of the pugaree. A troop consisted of from thirty to fifty men.

Having been supplied with a Martini-Henry rifle and fifty rounds of ammunition, I was now fully equipped, and the next day I went out, in all the glory of my new uniform, to meet the mule-wagon. My improved appearance made such an impression on Grant that he lost no time in enlisting, and was enrolled the same day.

After three months in this troop of police, I joined the Africander Corps, which was a body of irregulars attached to them under Captain Van Niekerk. As they were composed of experienced men, well acquainted with the country and accustomed to savage warfare, I thought there would be a much better chance of seeing some of the fighting.

We were scouting in the outlying district, where the Matabele had been seen, but although we got into touch with them here and there, we had no serious engagement. Later on we were sent out on the Shangani Patrol, visiting the district where Major Wilson and his party were cut up during the first Matabele War.

This patrol numbered from two hundred to three hundred police, with the mounted infantry of the Yorks and Lancs Regiment, a detachment of the 7th Hussars, under Colonel Paget—with whom was Prince Alexander of Teck—and a battalion of infantry.

The natives were lodged in the hills, and from a position of comparative safety were able to pour in a galling fire on the troops, while we were unable to inflict any serious loss on them in return. However, we lost only a few men killed, but had several deaths from fever.

The man who gave us the greatest trouble was a chief named Umwini, who was the leader of the rebellion in that district. I was present on several occasions at *indabas* (*indaba* is the native word for a meeting to discuss any matter), when he would come out of his stronghold and stand on the rocks in full view of us; but when asked to surrender, he replied contemptuously that we were a lot of boys and that he would never be taken by us.

His kraal was high up amongst some almost inaccessible crags on the mountain side, and all efforts failed to dislodge him, until a few of the Dutch Corps, of whom I was one, managed to steal upon him unawares. We reached his cave in the early dawn, and saw him, through the opening, sitting, with only a few of his followers, round some lighted candles which he had probably looted from one of the stores. One of our men, taking careful aim, shot him through the shoulder, and then, rushing the cave, we took him prisoner. He was tried by a court martial, and sentenced to be shot, and when the time came for the sentence to be carried out he showed himself a thoroughly brave man, refusing to be blindfolded or to stand with his back to the firing party, saying that he wished to see death coming.

It was about this time that I first met B.-P.—now General Sir R. S. S. Baden-Powell, but then only Colonel—who had been sent up to take charge of the operations, and who confirmed the court martial's sentence on Umwini. I was on water guard that day, to see that the natives did not poison the stream, when a man whom I took for a trooper came up and entered into conversation with me, asking about my past experiences, &c., and it was only when I got back to camp, after going off duty, that I found I had been talking to the officer in command of the expedition.

A general plan of attack was now organised, under the direction of Colonel Baden-Powell, and the natives were finally dislodged from the hills and the rebellion crushed.

On the successful termination of the patrol a fort was built at Umvunga Drift, where I remained for some time; but it was a most unhealthy place, nearly every man going down, sooner or later, with fever and dysentery. There was absolutely no medicine of any sort in the place, and we consequently lost several men. I myself had a bad attack of dysentery, but managed to cure it by making a very thin mixture with my ration of flour and some water, which I drank daily until the attack was cured.

In the centre of the fort stood a big tree, and after cutting away the branches at the top we erected a platform on the trunk, which, besides serving as a look-out, made a splendid platform for a Maxim gun which we mounted there, and were thus able to command the surrounding country within range.

During my stay here we had one or two brushes with the natives, but they gradually settled down; so, on a relief force being sent up, I returned to Bulawayo, where the corps was disbanded. I then got a post as one of the guard over a number of murderers lying in Bulawayo goal awaiting sentence, all of whom were finally hanged.

In the course of the twelve months that I remained in Bulawayo I made the acquaintance of a man named Elstop, who is mentioned by Mr. F. C. Selous in one of his books. This man was one of the oldest hands in the country, and had been one of the pioneers in Rhodesia, and had also spent a good deal of time trading and storekeeping among the natives of the interior.

It was my acquaintance with him that finally decided me on my future course of action. The tales he told of his experiences in the earlier days, when elephants and other game were to be met with in plenty, fired my blood, and I said that I wished I had been in the country at that time. He said that I should probably find the same state of things still existing farther north. This was quite enough for me, and I resolved to find out for myself if he was right.

I was then in partnership with a man named Frielich, carrying on business as fruit and produce merchants, under the name of the Colonial Fruit and Produce Stores of Bulawayo. I had put practically all my savings into the business, but this did not alter my resolution to go north, and by mutual agreement we dissolved partnership.

I have since learned that Frielich finally made over £100,000 out of the business. Before the Boer War broke out he had stored an immense amount of forage, which he was able to sell during the war at his own price, and so amassed a comfortable fortune, in which, of course, had I stayed in Bulawayo, I should have shared.

Before starting out on our new venture I thought I would take a short holiday at the seaside; so going down to East London, in Cape Colony, I joined some men I had met during the Matabele War, and we stayed there some time, camping out on the sands.

Finding that the funds were running out, I took to the sea again, and, getting a ship, worked my way round to Durban. Here I had to look round again for something to do, and finding that a Shakespearian company was playing in the town at the time, I presented myself at the stage manager's office and applied for an engagement. They happened to have a vacancy, and I was taken on for small parts. The company was at rehearsal when I was engaged, and I was told to take my place at once among the others on the stage. As far as I could judge, I was no worse than the other members of the company, and for a month I appeared nightly for the edification of the aristocracy of Durban.

Tiring of the stage, I again took to the sea, and worked my way, from port to port, round to Zanzibar, where I gathered all the information I could about the interior, which did not amount to much more than that the country was very wild indeed.

However, my mind was made up now, and I was not to be scared off my plan; so, as there were no boats running to Mombasa—which is the gateway of British East Africa—I bargained with an Arab for a passage on a dhow which carried native passengers between the various ports along the coast. The owner of the dhow provided no accommodation for his passengers, and I suppose one could hardly expect that he would, seeing that the fare from Zanzibar to Mombasa—a distance of about 250 miles—was only two rupees, or two shillings and eightpence!

The boat had a single mast, and carried one huge sail. It had no compass or lights, and was navigated round the coast by keeping as close inshore as possible all the time. There was no place to make a fire or any provision for cooking. It had been so, the Arab told me, in the days of his father, and what was good enough for his father was good enough for him and those who chose to travel with him. This was said in Arabic, but was translated to me by a fellow-passenger who could speak a little English.

With fully fifty people on board the tiny craft we started on our voyage along the coast, but had not gone very far before we were in trouble. With the huge sail set to catch the breeze, we were flying merrily along, when we were suddenly brought up all standing, and found that we had come across some obstacle in the water. We were very quickly informed what it was by a shouting crowd of excited native fishermen who swarmed round our boat, loudly demanding to be compensated for the damage done to their nets, which, it seemed, formed the obstacle that had pulled us up and which we had destroyed.

The owner of the dhow did not seem to be at all disposed to give in to their demands, and they were about to seize the small boat which we were towing behind us, when I thought it was time to take a hand in the argument, as, in case of any accident to the dhow, this boat was our only hope of safety, the waters in that part being said to be infested with sharks. Picking up an axe, which happened to be lying handy, I jumped into the boat and threatened to brain the first man who came within reach. Although they did not understand English, my attitude was evidently suggestive enough to make it clear that they were safer at a distance, and, realizing that they were not likely to get any satisfaction by continuing the argument, they allowed us to proceed on our way.

After this we made fairly good headway, with a favourable wind, and, occupied in watching the changing scenery opening out as we made our way along the coast, I had almost forgotten the incident. I was settling down to enjoy the trip when, without any warning, we were suddenly pulled up again with a jerk, and the dhow came to a fullstop again.

Every one immediately got into a wild state of excitement, shouting and gesticulating, and making a perfect pandemonium of noise. The captain was shouting as wildly as the rest, and, thinking he was giving orders, I was surprised to see that nobody attempted to carry them out, but on asking the passenger who could speak some English what orders he was giving, and why no one obeyed them, he said, " He is not giving orders, he is praying. He is calling on Allah to help him." This was no use to me, and I thought the best thing I could do was to take charge myself; so, getting the man to whom I had spoken to act as interpreter, I told them what to do to put things right. They then calmed down a good deal, and I went to take soundings. There was no leadline on board, so I had to make one with some old iron and some pieces of rope that were lying about. On sounding I found plenty of water on one side of the ship, while on the other it was very shallow, so that we were evidently stuck on a reef. As soon as I was certain of this I lashed some rope to the anchor, and had it taken out about twenty or thirty yards from the ship, in the small boat, and then dropped overboard. Then I made everybody lend a hand to pull hard on the rope, and after about six hours' hard work we managed to pull her off. In case of trouble I kept the axe handy, but they were ready enough to obey my orders, so nothing happened.

When we got her off I found that the dhow was leaking pretty badly, so everybody was kept busy baling out the water, while I took the helm, and, keeping her close in to the land, steered towards Mombasa.

Noticing a large white building on the shore, I asked what it was, and my interpreter told me that it was the residence of a white man, and that the place was called Shimoni; so I took the boat in as close as possible and dropped anchor. On landing I found that the house was occupied by a British official, who offered to put me up, so I stayed the night there. The next morning I found that the dhow had continued her journey, and, as Mombasa was only thirty miles from Shimoni, I walked the rest of the way.

Mombasa is the starting-point of the Uganda Railway, of which so much has already been written. At the time of my arrival the railway was only in the initial stages of its construction, and just beginning to stretch its track through the almost unknown interior of British East Africa. So far it had only advanced a comparatively short distance into the Protectorate, and from the very start the engineers were faced at every step with some of the numerous difficulties which lie in the way of railway building in a new and savage country, from men and animals, as well as from the climate and tropical vegetation. The loss of life from wild animals, as well as from the climate, was very heavy.

In those days the European quarter of Mombasa was only a small cluster of buildings—chiefly Government offices—with one hotel, which was kept by a Greek. Two or three Europeans trading in the interior had stores here, and the British Government was represented by a Sub-Commissioner.

Mombasa—meaning Isle of War—is of great interest to the student of history. It is situated on an island, connected to the mainland by a bridge. There is a huge native town and an old Portuguese fort, several hundred years old, built in the days of Henry the Navigator, in whose reign the Portuguese ships visited all the ports of the known world, and many others, till then unknown.

Thinking that I should be most likely to get the information I required from the Government, I called on the Sub-Commissioner, and asked him to advise me as to the best way of carrying out my plan of visiting the interior. Very much to my surprise, I was received with the scantest courtesy, and given very plainly to understand that white men, whether travellers or hunters, were by no means welcome. They were not wanted, he told me, under any circumstances, and he advised me to leave the country at once.

CHAPTER III

I OWN I was a little discouraged by this reception, but it did not alter my determination to remain— in spite of the veiled threat of the official to prevent my going up-country; so I set out to make a few inquiries for myself.

I found that there were a number of caravans going up to Uganda, the main road to which place was protected by a line of forts, placed about a hundred miles apart. North and south of this caravan road the country was practically unknown, being under no administration, and chiefly inhabited by hostile tribes.

A mutiny had recently broken out among the troops in Uganda, on account of which the whole country was in disorder, and a lot of transport was required in the disaffected district. Here, again, I thought I saw my opportunity.

At that time everything had to be carried upon the heads of native porters, so that each load, averaging about sixty pounds in weight, was costing from sixty to one hundred rupees—very often a lot more than the value of the goods carried—before it reached its destination.

I was convinced that this state of things could be improved on; and chancing to meet a man named Gibbons—a white trader—as I left the Commissioner, I talked over the question of cheapening the cost of transport with him, and we finally decided that it could be done by using donkeys and wagons in the place of porters; so we decided to try the scheme in partnership.

Having settled the bargain, we set to work to prepare the expedition. Altogether we purchased about thirty donkeys, which cost us about a hundred rupees each, and got as many wagons as we thought sufficient. In the meantime I set to work to make the harness, as we could not get any in Mombasa, and by using rope and sacking I managed to turn out a sufficient number of very creditable sets.

We also decided to take a hundred porters with us in case of accident, as our contract provided for a heavy fine if we did not deliver the goods on time. These porters were chiefly Swahili, a name meaning "coast dwellers." These Swahili consider themselves more civilized than the people of the interior. They practise the Mohammedan religion and copy the Arabs in their dress. Swahili porters march under a headman of their own race, who receives his orders and repeats them to his followers. If, as sometimes happens, there are porters from other native tribes in the caravan, each tribe has its representative headman. For each ten carriers there is an *askari*, or soldier, who is armed with a rifle, and whose duty it is to keep guard at night and protect the caravan on the road. These askaris also act as police and keep order generally, and bring in any deserters. As may be easily imagined, it would hardly do to trust merely to the askaris' sense of duty for the prevention of desertion, but a clearly understood condition of their engagement in that capacity ensures their using their best endeavours to prevent anything of the sort. It is the recognized rule on all *safaris* that, if any man of the ten in an askari's section deserts, and the askari cannot bring him back, he will himself have to carry the deserter's load for the rest of the journey. Apart from the unpleasantness of having to carry a sixty-pound load in the ranks of the porters instead of swaggering along with no other burden than his rifle, ammunition, and blanket, the blow to his self-importance involved in the degradation from askari to porter is one that would be severely felt by any nigger, who is probably blessed with more self-esteem than even a circus-ring master or a newly appointed Sub-Commissioner, and the fear of such degradation is a wonderful spur on the askaris' watchfulness. A cook and a private servant completed the outfit.

On this occasion we had two hundred loads of Government goods to take up to Uganda, and one hundred loads of trade goods which we were taking up on our own account, our intention being to deliver the Government goods at their destination and then start on a private trading and hunting expedition away up north, in the direction of Lake Rudolph, where we hoped to buy more donkeys, as we had heard that they were very cheap in that district.

Having completed all our arrangements, we put the whole caravan—men, donkeys, wagons, and loads—on the train, and started for railhead, which was then about 150 miles from Mombasa. This was in the year 1898. On arriving safely at the terminus of the line we left the train and went into camp.

We found that the district around us was infested with lions, whose ferocity had created such a state of panic among the Indian coolies working on the construction of the line that the work had practically stopped. No less than thirty of the coolies had been carried off by them, and I found the remainder sleeping in the trees and afraid to go to work.

Many stories were told of the audacity of the lions, who prowled round the camp nightly, and rarely left without one or more victims. In one case an Irishman, named O'Hara, who had charge of the coolies engaged in the construction of the line, set himself to watch for the man-eater, in the hope of getting a shot at him, and took his post with his rifle by the door of his tent, in which his wife was sleeping. The night passed without incident, and towards morning he must have dozed off, for his wife awakened to see him being dragged off into the bush by a lion. His mutilated body was eventually found by the search party within a short distance of the camp.

On another occasion three men with whom I was personally well acquainted had a remarkable experience. They were watching for lions from a railway carriage—a construction wagon on the line—the door of which they left open. Two of them, Perenti and Hubner, made themselves as comfortable as they could on rugs laid on the floor of the carriage to rest till their turn for watching came, while the third, a man named Rial, took up a position near the door, where he evidently fell asleep. A prowling lion scented the party, and took a flying leap into the carriage. The impact of his landing made the carriage oscillate, and swung the door to, caging the whole party and their unwelcome guest. Perenti told me that he was awakened by the curious smell of the lion, and, putting out his hand, felt the animal standing over him. Directly he was touched the beast let out a terrific roar, and, seizing Rial by the throat, sprang clean through the window with him and made off. The body, partly eaten, was found in the bush next morning.

Some of the dodges to kill the lions had distinctly humorous results, and I remember being much amused with the story of one man's experience. I must explain that to provide the labourers with water,

tanks were placed beside the line, which were refilled
at intervals. One genius had the idea of lying in
wait for lions in one of these tanks, in one side of
which he made a hole in which to insert the barrel
of his rifle—quite overlooking the fact that the lion
might prefer to approach from the opposite side,
which was what actually happened. The animal,
scenting him, immediately knocked the lid off the
tank and tried to fish him out with his paw. He
was unable to get his rifle round, and could only
shrink into the smallest possible space in the corner
of the tank—fortunately beyond the reach of the lion
—and remain quiet until the beast was driven off. He
was lucky enough to escape with a torn blanket and
a few deep scratches where the lion had just managed
to reach him with his claws. Of course, he had to
endure a considerable amount of chaff on the result
of his original attempt at lion-hunting.

I myself had a narrow escape before leaving railhead, for which the lions were indirectly responsible.
I had been dining with one of the railway officials,
and had stayed rather late, it being after ten o'clock
when I set out to return to my own camp. Not expecting to be out so late, I had not brought my rifle,
so, as it was of course pitch dark, I took a blazing
brand from the camp fire, and started to walk the
two miles to my own place. After going for some
time I saw some fires in the distance, and, thinking
they were those of my own people, I made towards
them. All at once I heard a terrific din of shouting
and beating of empty paraffin-cans. While wondering what on earth all the row was about I heard
firing, and some shots whizzed past, unpleasantly
close to my head. Dropping flat, I began shouting,
and the firing presently ceased. I was then able to
make my way into camp, which I found was one
made for some of the Indian coolies, who had mistaken the light of my firebrand for the eye of a lion.
I was persuaded to stay the remainder of the night in

their *boma* and return to my own camp in the morning. A *boma*, or *zareba* as it is called in the Soudan, is a rough fence of thorn-bushes or brushwood built round a camp to keep prowlers, whether two or four footed, at a distance.

We were all very busy now, getting the wagons and harness ready and fixing up the loads for our journey to Uganda.

We found that if we were to get the loads through by the time agreed upon we should want at least five hundred porters, so we tried to engage some natives from the Wakamba [1] to go with us. With the native disinclination to move except just as they felt inclined, they absolutely refused to go; so it was arranged that I should go on ahead with the wagons, while Gibbons should come on later with the porters.

I started with one hundred loads of Government stuff on five wagons, while my camp outfit, food &c., was carried on another, and took about twenty of the men with me. Being unable to get the necessary porters, we had to leave some of the loads behind in charge of two of the men, intending to return for them later, but, as it happened, we never saw them again.

I soon found that the donkey outfit did not work by any means as smoothly as we had hoped, the donkeys never having been in harness before and the men being new to the work. The drivers could not keep on the road, wagons capsized, and things went wrong generally. None of the rivers we had to cross were bridged, and when we had got the wagons down into the hollow of the river bed it was a terrible job to get them up on the other side; the only way being to get all the boys to push at the back, so that it took several hours' hard work at each of the rivers

---

[1] Wakamba, *i.e.*, natives of the Kamba tribe who inhabit that region.

before we managed to get donkeys, wagons, and loads from one side to the other.

The country generally was dry and bushy, being covered with thick scrub, which made our progress so slow that, after two or three days' travelling, we were overtaken by Gibbons with the remainder of the men.

While we were sitting by the camp fire that night, waiting for a meal, I was very nearly shot by Gibbons, who was anxious to explain the working of the Snider rifle to me. Taking a rifle from an askari, he put in a cartridge, wishing to show me that it was absolutely impossible for it to go off at half-cock, and, pointing the rifle towards me, he said, " You see, it won't go off now." I objected, and was pushing the rifle to one side, when it actually did go off, the bullet whizzing close by my ear!

The free, gipsy-like life in the open just suited my inclination. The absolute freedom to go where one liked, and do as one liked, without any of the restrictions which meet one on every side in civilized countries, and the feeling that you are literally " monarch of all you survey," appealed very strongly to me, and I felt that I had at last found the life suited thoroughly to my disposition.

We started off again and made very good progress, as, by the aid of the moon, we were able to travel at night. We were now crossing the Athi Plain, which extends for about one hundred miles and teems with almost every kind of game except elephants, so we were able to keep the caravan well supplied with meat. Almost every night my boys used to rouse me up with a scare of lions, but, although I always turned out I never saw any cause for the excitement.

After travelling for some days, we finally arrived at Nairobi, since become the capital of British East Africa, and here the character of the country completely changed. From the dry scrub-covered plain we now entered a splendid grazing country, with magnificent forests and beautiful woodland scenery, making a very pleasant change from the bare landscape of the last few marches. What is now known as Nairobi was then practically a swamp, and from the nature of the surrounding country I should never have imagined that it would be chosen as the site for the future capital of British East Africa. Indeed, I still think that by going a little farther westward a situation far more suitable in every way would have been found. The town of Nairobi takes its name from a river of the same name which rises in the neighbouring hills, the river forming the boundary-line between the Masai and Kikuyu countries, and the plain where the town now stands was at this time an absolutely uninhabited district, without a village of any kind. We outspanned for the night on the edge of the swamp which borders the present town. Being thoroughly tired out with the day's work, I was resting in my tent, when about six o'clock in the afternoon I heard my boys calling me with one of the usual stories about lions being about. Finding that they seemed more excited than usual, I turned out to see if there really was any cause for alarm, and saw two lions stalking the donkeys in the gathering dusk. They came quite close up to the camp, and I then saw that one was a lioness, so, having heard that if the female were shot the male would clear off, while if the male were shot the female became savage, and would probably attack, I fired at the female and thought I hit her, though, owing to the bad light and the fact that my gun—a Martini-Metford—was a very poor one, and could not be relied on to shoot straight, I could not be certain. The animals turned and plunged into the swamp, but though we saw signs of blood and tracked them for some distance, we had to give up on account of the gathering darkness, and the next morning we could find no signs of them.

Some of the Masai tribe were in the neighbourhood, and visited our camp. This was the first time I had come across any of this race, of whom so much has been written, and I was naturally very much interested. They seemed very friendly, and, in spite of their warlike reputation, we had no trouble with them at all. Physically, they were very fine specimens of the African native, and certainly make very good fighting-men.

We were about to enter the practically unknown country of the Kikuyu tribe, a people whose reputation was such that only the most daring of the white traders would even venture to set foot over the boundary, and then only at the greatest risk of their lives and goods.

Those who only know the Kikuyu people as they are to-day may find some difficulty in crediting many of the statements I shall make as to their character and reputation at the time when I spent some three or four very lively years among them, but a short quotation from the late Sir Gerald Portal's book on the " British Mission to Uganda in 1893," dealing with the race as they were then—which accurately describes them as I found them five years later—may help the doubting ones to a clearer realization of the facts.

Describing the British East Africa Company's station, Fort Smith,[1] in the Kikuyu country, Sir Gerald says :—

" The Kikuyu tribes were practically holding the Company's station in a state of siege." Later on he says : " We left the open plain and plunged into the darkness of a dense belt of forest, which forms the natural boundary of the regions inhabited by the treacherous, cunning, and usually hostile people of Kikuyu. Warned by the state of affairs which we had

---

[1] Fort Smith was situated close to where the present town of Nairobi now stands.

heard was prevailing at the Company's fort in this
district, we were careful to keep all our people close
together, every man within a couple of paces of his
neighbour. One European marched in front, one in
the rear, and one in the middle of the long line. The
Wa-Kikuyu, as we knew, seldom or never show themselves, or run the risk of a fight in the open, but lie
like snakes in the long grass, or in some dense bush
within a few yards of the line of march, watching
for a gap in the ranks, or for some incautious porter
to stray away, or loiter a few yards behind; even
then not a sound is heard; a scarcely perceptible
' twang ' of a small bow, the almost inaudible
' whizz ' of a little poisoned arrow for a dozen yards
through the air, a slight puncture in the arm, throat,
or chest, followed, almost inevitably, by the death of
a man. Another favourite trick of the Wa-Kikuyu
is to plant poisoned skewers in the path, set at an
angle of about forty-five degrees, pointing towards
the direction from which the stranger is expected.
If the path is much overgrown or hidden by the
luxuriant growth of long grass, these stakes are of
much greater length and so pointed that they would
pierce the stomach of any one advancing towards
them.[1] Keeping a sharp look-out for these delicate
attentions, our progress was inevitably slow, but at
length we arrived without further adventure at the
strong stockade, ditch, brick houses, and well-
guarded stores known as Fort Smith in Kikuyu,
above which was floating the Company's flag.

" Outside the Fort itself the state of affairs was not
so pleasant to contemplate. We were surrounded day
and night by a complete ring of hostile Wa-Kikuyu,
hidden in the long grass and bushes, and for any

---

[1] Sir Gerald was evidently misinformed on this
point, as I ascertained during my stay in the country
that it had never been the custom to use long stakes
such as he describes.

one to wander alone for more than two hundred yards from the stockade was almost certain death. On the morning of our arrival, a porter of Martin's caravan, who had strayed down to the long grass at the foot of the little hill on which the station is built, was speared through the back and killed within 250 paces of our tents. A short time before eight soldiers in the Company's service who were foraging for food —probably in an illicit manner—were all massacred in a neighbouring village; and a day or two before our arrival the natives had even had the temerity to try and set fire to the fort itself at night.

" It will, however, be a matter of time and difficulty, requiring great tact, patience, and firmness, to induce these Wa-Kikuyu to have confidence in Europeans, and to discontinue their practice of spearing or otherwise murdering any defenceless Swahili porter whom they may find straying away by himself.

"Long before I went to their country myself I remember being told by an African traveller of great renown that the only way in which to deal with the Kikuyu people, whether singly or in masses, was to ' shoot at sight.' "

The Martin mentioned by Sir Gerald Portal above was one of the pioneers of British East Africa. He was a Maltese sailor, who came to this country with Joseph Thompson, and was the first white man to venture among the Masai. He now manages the Mabira forest rubber estate.

Another traveller, Mr. G. F. Scott Elliott, speaking of the Kikuyu in his book, " A Naturalist in Mid Africa," says : " They are only too anxious to spear a lagging porter."[1] He also describes the murder by these people of forty-nine out of fifty men composing an Arab or Swahili trading caravan.

[1] For further reference to the Kikuyu tribe see Professor Gregory's excellent book " The Great Rift Valley," 1896.

Later on I was destined to be the first white man
to live amongst this pleasant people, enter into their
daily life, and bring them into something like close
touch with European civilization.

We were warned to be very careful when we
reached the Kikuyu country, and to keep a good
guard, as they had a very bad name, being very
treacherous and not to be trusted in any way; but,
keeping a sharp look-out, we passed the boundary
without any interference from them. We kept to the
caravan road, which passed along the outskirts of
the country, as we were told that every caravan
going through the country had had trouble with the
natives, having had porters killed and goods stolen.

About this time Gibbons left me and pushed on
ahead, as we were anxious to get the loads through,
while, the surrounding country being splendid grazing ground, I remained about a week to give the
animals a rest before crossing the practically uninhabited district which lay between my present camp
and the ravine—the station on the road to Uganda
for which I was bound.

Being short of donkeys, some having died on the
road, I decided to redistribute the loads, and make the
total weight somewhat less by leaving some of my
personal belongings behind. Among the things I left
was my tent. This I had good cause to regret later
on. We had been gradually rising nearly all the
way as we approached the high escarpment of the
Kedong Valley, which is about five thousand feet
above sea-level, and therefore very cold, and the absence of my tent caused me considerable discomfort.

Arriving at the top of the escarpment and looking
down the precipitous slope on the farther side, the
first question was how we were to get the wagons
down into the valley, where we could see a number
of Masai villages, the road being very narrow and
full of holes, besides being plentifully strewn with
boulders.

I decided to camp at the top for the night and make a start early the next morning. That night on the top of the mountain taught me a lesson—never again to travel without my tent. Besides the discomfort of the cold, there is always the danger of getting a dose of fever, and this was what I did on the present occasion.

Rousing the camp at a very early hour, we set to work to devise some means of getting the caravan down the side of the escarpment. There were no brakes on the wagons, and the donkeys would not go down even without the wagons unless they were absolutely driven. So, to get the wagons down, I tried a plan of my own, which, at the first attempt, came very near to killing me.

Taking the donkeys out of the wagon, I placed a boy on each side with a rope to ease it down, while I took hold of the shaft. When it went too fast, I told the boys to put stones under the wheels to check the pace, and so let it down gradually. As I had already shown them how to place stones at the back of the wheels in coming up the hill to prevent the wagon running back, I thought that they would have the sense to see that the stones must be put in front when going down hill. The result impressed upon me the fact that the nigger cannot argue from analogy, but that everything you wish him to do must be carefully explained in the fullest detail.

We got along all right until the hill-side began to get very steep, and I found the boys could not hold the wagon. They started to let go, and I shouted to them to get the stones in place. Their stupidity would have been laughable if my position had not been so serious. Instead of putting the stones in front of the wheels, they put them at the back, as they had been taught to do when we were getting the wagons up the hill, and seemed surprised when the wagon ran away from the stones, and before I could make them understand what I wanted, the boys at the ropes had let go. Being unable to let go myself, I had to hang on like grim death, while the wagon went tearing down the slope. One minute I was bumping on the road and the next I was in the air, with trees and other things whizzing past. By making the best use of my chances when my feet touched the ground, I managed to keep the wagon on the road until very near the bottom of the hill, when it ran over a hole and capsized. Luckily very little damage was done, but it took us the whole day to get all the wagons and animals down, and when we camped at night every one was thoroughly tired out with the hard day's work.

The valley was very fertile, and made a splendid grazing ground for cattle, the Masai regularly bringing their stock there to graze at certain seasons of the year, and at the time of our arrival a large number of them were camping on the spot with their herds of stock.

While out shooting one day in the valley, one of my porters showed me the spot where he said a trader named Dick, with five or six hundred of his men, had been murdered by the Masai. Dick himself had shot seventeen of his assailants before he was killed. I went to examine the ground, and found it covered with so large a number of skulls and bones that I was inclined to think that the boy had used less than the usual native amount of exaggeration in telling the story. So far as I know, no attempt has ever been made to punish the Masai for this massacre. Another of the porters, on my asking him how he had lost an eye, told me that it had been torn out by the Masai—formerly a common practice of theirs when they caught any Arab or Swahili traders passing through their country. They were habitually very offensive to strangers, generally forcing them to camp a considerable distance from water, which they then proceeded to make them buy, their practice being to stick a spear into the ground, and make the trader pay in goods, brass and iron wire, and beads, as the case might be, to the height of the spear, before they would let him pass.

As I have said, there were a number of Masai in the valley, but I had no trouble with them; many of them came into camp with milk, which I bought from them. I found that it had a distinctly smoky taste, due to the gourds in which it is carried being hung over the fire to clean them.

The Masai always seemed well disposed towards me, and, as is their custom when they wish to be polite, paid me the compliment of spitting on their hands before shaking hands with me. The bearing of the *elmoran*, or warriors, was certainly truculent and insulting, but I managed not to give offence, and even succeeded in trading with them for a few donkeys to replace those of mine which had died on the road, and one which had been killed by a hyena; and when the animals were sufficiently rested, we were able to resume our journey to Lake Naivasha, where there is a Government station, without further incident of note.

The natives along the Uganda Road were now beginning to get accustomed to the altered state of things. Caravans were going through the country regularly, and they had sense enough to understand that the white man had come to stay, and any attempt to oppose his coming would probably have serious consequences for themselves, resulting in the loss of their herds and their best grazing-grounds. Of course they did not realize all this at once. The old fighting spirit of the warriors could not be entirely checked in a moment, but it was only in isolated instances that they dared to attack the white intruders; they had always been accustomed to make war on the neighbouring tribes as they pleased, and up to recent years would raid portions of British East African territory, and make organized descents into German East Africa. To the present day they will carry off cattle whenever the opportunity offers, arguing that, as the original owners of all the cattle in the country, they are perfectly within their rights in helping themselves.

Two or three days later we camped by the side of Lake Elmenteita, where I had a curious experience with a lion. It had been my custom to give out rations about once a week, but my men had exchanged their flour with the Masai for milk, and we had run short of food, so I said I would go and shoot them some meat. As I had practically run out of ammunition also, I took only two or three rounds out with me, and these I had fired off without result, with the exception of the one round which it is usual to keep in case of emergency. On the way back to camp I saw a zebra, which I thought would be just the thing for the men, so I started to crawl on hands and knees towards an ant-hill which was about fifty yards from the zebra, thinking that from there I could get him with one shot. With my rifle in one hand, and the cartridge in the other, I had reached the ant-hill, and was just looking round the corner to get a shot at the zebra, when I saw a lion about two yards off looking straight at me. He was evidently after the zebra too, and the meeting was a pretty big surprise for both of us. It is one thing to go out hunting a lion, but quite another to meet one unexpectedly round a corner in this way, and I was so taken aback that I could not find the cartridge. I was far too surprised to be scared, and started fumbling in my pockets and about my clothes to find the cartridge which I held in my hand; the lion also seemed to think there was something curious about the affair, as, after looking at me for a few seconds, he walked quietly away, before I discovered the cartridge in my hand. By this time the zebra had also gone, and with it the last chance of any meat that night.

The next day I got plenty of meat for the boys.

and continuing to follow the caravan road, we moved on as far as Lake Nakuru, and from there to Equator Camp—so called from its being situated exactly on the Equator—where we halted.   Two days later we reached the Ravine, where I handed over my loads at the Government Fort.   There had been a mutiny of native troops and the Ravine was the only station which had not been taken over by the mutineers.   I ought really to have gone on up to Uganda, but the rains were on, and it was very difficult to get through with the wagons, and as I was feeling very ill, I was relieved from going through to my proper destination.

At Ravine Fort I met Major Smith, after whom Fort Smith was named, and found him a very interesting man.   He was an ex-Life Guardsman, and had had a very interesting career in the early days of British East Africa, and had lost one hand in the course of his adventures.   I also met Martin, whom I have already mentioned in the extract from Sir Gerald Portal's book with reference to the Kikuyu.

My partner, Gibbons, had gone on to Uganda, where he would deliver the other loads, being able to get through more easily with porters than I with wagons, so I thought that my best plan would be to return to railhead—which would be about three hundred miles back from the Ravine—and make arrangements about the loads we had left behind, and also secure more transport.

I had very little food for my men on the return journey, and was unable to buy any at the Ravine, as their supply had run short through trouble with the Nandi natives.   So we started out with a very poor prospect in front of us, and I myself was really not well enough to do anything.   The men, too, not having been accustomed to the donkey wagons, were dissatisfied with the class of work they had been doing for me, and all the flour having given out, they were evidently anxious to get away.   I was not much surprised, therefore, when, having turned in early one night, feeling far from well, I woke the next morning to find that every one of my men had deserted. This was at Equator Camp.

No one who has not experienced it can realize the feeling of being left absolutely alone in the wilds, with everything on your hands. Certainly I did not find it a pleasant one, and the fact that I was ill did not lighten my troubles. I made up my mind not to be beaten, however, and set myself to make the best of a bad job. Thinking that if I could overtake the men I might induce some of them to return, I went out for some distance, but not seeing anything of them, returned to the lonely camp. Before setting out after the men I had untied all the donkeys, and at night I had no difficulty in finding them again, and having tied them up as usual, I made a big fire round them and settled down to rest as well as I could. I slept through the night without being disturbed, and turned out early in the morning, having thought out the previous night what I should do. Not wishing to abandon the wagons, I tied them together, one behind the other, and put all the donkeys in front, inspanned on the leading wagon. Having fixed the caravan up like this I started off, and an awful time I had of it. Sometimes the road would turn, and then the job was to get the wagons round the bend without capsizing—which I could not always do, and by the time I had righted the wagons the donkeys would be all mixed up. I started off at six in the morning, and travelled until three o'clock in the after-noon, by which time I had reached the Njora River, where I halted, and managed to shoot a buck and had a good meal, which I thoroughly enjoyed, having been all day without food. Tying up the donkeys, I turned in and had a well-earned rest.

Feeling better for this, I started off early the next morning, and soon came across a solitary nigger, whom I commandeered. He was a stray porter, who had evidently deserted from some caravan, and was nearly starving. I gave him some meat, which he seemed uncommonly glad to get, and we went on together. We had a pretty long trek that day, and the next morning we started off again as soon as it was light for another long march, as it was thirty miles to the next camp where we could get water, and what with the delay caused by wagons capsizing, and trouble with the donkeys, it was ten o'clock at night before I got in. I arrived at my halting-place alone, my native follower having slipped quietly away into the darkness, and I never saw him again. I had brought same water with me in a bucket, but the jolting of the wagon had upset it, and having had no food all day, and suffering from the want of water, I was absolutely dead beat. The first thing I did was to outspan the donkeys and let them have a feed; then I took a bucket and went to look for water. The water-hole was about a mile away, and as it was pitch dark I had no easy job to find it. However, I succeeded at last, and just as I got there I was startled by something jumping up and brushing right past me. I knew from the sharp growl that it must have been a lion which I had disturbed when drinking. I was too done up to pay much attention to it, and having satisfied my thirst, I half-filled my bucket with water and made my way back to camp, where I had some trouble to find enough wood to make a fire. Eventually I managed to get one going and turned in. Before turning in I had noticed a fire at some little distance, which I put down to natives, and when I turned out in the morning, after having satisfied myself that the donkeys had not been interfered with by lions, I started off in the direction in which I had seen the fire in the hope of being able to get some help. The camp proved to be that of some East Indians, who were taking food to a party of railway surveyors who were out ahead, and they supplied me with some rice and let me have a couple of boys, and with this assistance I got started again, and managing to pick up a few boys here and there, I finally reached railhead, after a tiresome and worrying journey.

My stay here was short, and I was soon on the road again, this time taking up food for the troops engaged in quelling the mutiny up in Uganda. Owing to the religious prejudices of the sepoys, all this food had to be brought from India, and transported from the coast by carriers, at a cost of two rupees per pound weight, so that it must have cost the Government at least 10s. per day to keep a private soldier in food alone, while, by comparison, the white officers were costing practically nothing, as they were able to live almost entirely on the country itself. My own experience convinces me that Indian troops are practically useless in Africa, owing to their not being able to live on the country, and I hold the same opinion with regard to the coolies working on the Uganda Railway, which I consider could have been built much more cheaply with white labour.

With the experience obtained on the previous trip, I had organized my safari for the second trip on different lines, being, among other things, careful to select my men from different tribes. When travelling in Africa, I have found it advisable never to get all the men from one tribe, as when the tribes are mixed they are less likely to mutiny or desert, or cause trouble in other ways. I also took care to have my tent with me on this trip, and when the caravan was ready to start I had, in addition to the donkey-wagons, about 120 native porters.

I might say here that the porters of East Africa, taking them all round, are a happy, careless lot. They will go through the greatest hardships on a journey, and on their return at once forget all their troubles in the pleasure of spending their wages as quickly as possible. They are chiefly Swahili, with a mixture of a few other tribes, such as the Wakamba.

The Masai, however, even to this day, will not lower themselves to carry loads.

I had by this time learned a little of the language, and had hopes that by the time I returned Gibbons would have got back, and we should be able to start on the journey we had originally planned. News travels quickly in Africa—indeed, with such remarkable speed as to be mysterious to the European mind —and I had heard that Gibbons was still up in Uganda, and later I received a letter to say that he was ill.

This question of the rapid transmission of news among the native races, both in Africa and India, has for a long time been a favourite subject for discussion and argument among white men who have had much to do with the native races. The well-known instances of the disaster to Hicks Pasha's force and the fall of Khartoum being known in the bazaars of Cairo long before any official intimation was received by the Government are cases in point. Personally, after fifteen years spent in close association with natives in Africa, I have absolutely no belief in the theory of any superhuman agency being employed. In the first place, there is always the fact that much of this wonderfully transmitted news is false, which discounts the value of such news generally and discredits its value though it turns out afterwards to be true. The white man who has sufficient experience of the nigger and his ways can generally winnow the grain of truth from the bushel of fiction with which it is wrapped about; while in the next place it must be borne in mind that the natives nearly all have recognized methods of passing news quickly from one point to another, of which I may mention a few.

The Kikuyu shouts his news from hill to hill, while the Masai runner thinks no more of carrying a message sixty miles in a day than we should of a three-mile stroll : the Congolese have a system of whistle signals, by which they can convey messages from one end of a district to the other in a very short time; while the West African native tells his news from village to village by means of a sort of Morse code, tapped out on drums. The Matabele uses a system of signalling by long and short obscurations of a fire, by means of a skin, or in daytime by long or short puffs of smoke regulated by the same means; while the Red Indian of North America was in the habit of using a similar method of communication. By these various methods it is quite possible to convey news enormous distances in a remarkably short space of time, and I think that they are quite sufficient to account for the many remarkable stories told of this sort of thing, without calling in the theory of any unknown agency at all.

I accomplished the trip with the food for the soldiers without any mishap, and began the return journey to railhead, travelling light, with nothing on the wagons; and having by this time become thoroughly used to the work, and knowing better how to handle the men, things went much more smoothly than on the previous trip.

The nights being cooler, and much more pleasant for travelling, we took advantage of the moonlight for our treks, resting during the daytime so that the donkeys could graze. There was something very fascinating about this moonlight travelling in the clear night air, with the stillness only broken by the sound of the wagon wheels and the patter of the donkeys' hoofs, whilst the long procession of black porters looked ghostly in the semi-darkness. Occasionally the surrounding silence would be broken by the sound of some wild animal disturbed by our approach, then all was quiet again.

As we were travelling light, it was not necessary to have all the donkeys inspanned in the wagons, and the spare animals were allowed to run loose alongside, stopping occasionally as they went along

to crop a few mouthfuls of grass, then trotting on
again to join the caravan. I was lying down on one
of the wagons, half dozing, one night, when I was
roused by the donkeys suddenly increasing their pace,
and looking up, I saw a lion stealthily approaching
one of the donkeys running loose by the roadside.
I immediately jumped off the wagon and called to
the men, but by this time the donkeys were all
bolting with fright, and it was only with a good deal
of difficulty that the wagons were stopped. By now
the lion I had first seen was nowhere in sight, but
another, probably his mate, was approaching the
donkeys from another direction. I could see him
coming leisurely along, evidently intent on a feed,
and I prepared to receive him. I had still the same
old gun, and having only a few cartridges, I waited
for the animal to approach near, so as to become as
good a target as possible. The brute had, so far,
been facing me, and as moonlight is deceptive, to
get a good shot I allowed him to come as close as I
thought advisable. Just as I was going to fire he
stopped, apparently uncertain what to make of the
situation, and as I hesitated for a moment he turned
slightly, and I fired immediately, and hit him in
the shoulder. With a savage growl, he gave a jump
into the air, and then began to tear up the ground
in a great rage. The sound of the report and the
growls of the lion again caused the donkeys to bolt,
which spoiled my aim for the second shot. I could
tell that I had wounded him severely, and thought
that I would go into camp, as I had intended, a little
farther on, and then return when daylight came and
find out whether I had really killed him. It was
about three o'clock when we camped, and we remained quiet for about two and a half hours waiting
until it was sufficiently light to go out again to
look for him. Going back to the spot where the
encounter had taken place, we found a large quantity
of blood, which showed that I had wounded him

severely, but the lion was not to be seen. After following the blood spoor for about a mile I saw the animal crouching in the scrub. We had been going very cautiously, and had got within about twenty yards of him, before we were made aware of his presence by a deep growl. Kneeling down and taking careful aim, I fired two or three shots, which I knew must have hit him by the thud of the bullet. Past experience had taught me not to approach too closely until certain that the brute was dead, as they are often most dangerous when you least expect it, so we waited some time before approaching the body, when we found that the last shots had really settled him. The boys skinned the carcass, and a great scramble ensued for the fat, which is greatly valued for certain healing properties it is supposed to possess. I know myself that it is a grand thing for rheumatism. The skin was brought back to the camp, at Lake Elmenteita, in triumph. This camp was known to the natives by the name of Camp Mabrook, from the fact that a big Arab trader named Mabrook, with all his safari, was murdered there while on his way up to Uganda.

My present safari I had equipped with the proceeds of my first trip to the Ravine, and as both trips had been successful, I was doing well. I had also heard from Gibbons that he was not coming back, and so the donkeys and wagons fell to me, as my share of the partnership.

My next contract was to carry rice for the porters accompanying the railway surveyors going from railhead up the Molo River, the distance being about the same as to the Ravine, but the road in this case branched off at Nakuru, going up more directly towards the Lake Victoria Nyanza.

As I was getting 30 rupees a load for this transport, and carrying 100 loads, I stood to make £200 on the journey, my expenses not being more than £50 for the trip. But it so happened that I was rather unlucky. Everything went well until I branched off at Nakuru, where I had to leave the caravan road and strike off across country. Here the road was so difficult for the wagons that I could only make a few miles each day. To add to our troubles, water was very scarce, and when we had travelled two days without finding any, both donkeys and men were exhausted, and I began to feel doubtful of getting through.

I had with me a couple of Masai who knew the country, and they assured me that we should find water not far away, but as we did not come to it as soon as they had led me to expect, I outspanned, and taking my rifle and one of the boys, I set off to find it.

In Africa one learns to judge from the formation of the country and the nature and state of the vegetation where one might expect to find water, and I was very successful in locating it, my judgment often proving right when the guides assured me that there was no water near. On this occasion it was nearly dark when we came to a swamp, and being terribly thirsty, we at once started drinking the dirty water, without stopping to look any farther, and, to our great disgust, afterwards found that there was a beautiful stream of running water only a few yards from where we had been drinking, which made us repent of our haste to quench our thirst. People who live in the civilized parts of the world can never really appreciate the true value of water. To the traveller in Africa it is the one thing he learns to prize above all others, and it is not surprising, therefore, to find the natives in some parts worshipping it as their god, since they know of no higher blessing.

Taking some of the water from the stream with us, we returned to camp and gave all the men a good drink, and early next morning I left the wagons, and took all the donkeys to have a good drink and a good

E

feed as well, as there was plenty of good grazing in the neighbourhood of the stream. The animals appeared to be thoroughly knocked up, and far from well, which I put down to their having been so long without water, though I was by no means sure that they had not been tampered with by the Masai drivers. The Masai are blood drinkers, and when they have a chance will make an incision in the jugular vein of an animal and thus drink its blood, and I had little doubt that this was what they had been doing to my donkeys while I was away looking for the water.

I brought up the wagons, and camped by the stream throughout the next day, as I saw that there was a good crossing over the stream, and the country was simply full of game. What struck me as most remarkable here was the tameness of the zebra, who were mixed up among my donkeys, all quietly grazing together near the wagons.

The condition of the donkeys began to get worse, and one by one they began to fall sick and die. Then the boys began to desert, as is the habit of the nigger when things begin to go wrong, and each day saw me with one donkey and one boy less.

It was part of my contract that the loads should be delivered by a certain time, otherwise I had to pay a heavy penalty—about two rupees a load for every twenty-four hours after the time fixed—so, as I had only some twenty-five miles farther to go, I set to work to collect the loads, intending to complete the rest of the journey without the wagons, by taking the rice on the donkeys' backs. By doing this I managed to get the journey completed and the loads delivered only a day or so after the proper time, but when I had finished the journey I found myself with just one donkey and three boys left!

It was impossible to take the wagons back without donkeys, so, taking the lid off one of the food boxes,

I painted on it with wagon grease " Dead Donkey Camp," and having stuck this up I left the wagons, and never saw them again, while with my three boys and my sole remaining donkey I started to trek back to Naivasha.

On the way back I met one or two parties surveying, who all complained of the difficulty of getting food, and said that their people were more or less starving. Rice was very difficult to get, as it had to be shipped to Mombasa and then brought up-country, while the cost of transport, as I have pointed out, was very heavy, and no food was to be got from the Nandi country, which lay between us and the Lake Victoria Nyanza.

Everybody knew that the Kikuyu country was full of food, but any parties which had gone out to buy supplies there had always been killed by the natives : in one instance a party had been attacked within about thirty miles of the Government station at Fort Smith, and nearly every man killed.

Food was wanted, I found, for the Government stations on the caravan road, as well as for the surveying parties on the line of the Uganda Railway, and as it was worth a rupee a pound, I thought I saw a good chance of making some money by trying my luck in the Kikuyu country.

Although I had lost all my wagons, I had not lost my desire for further adventure, and the opportunity of getting away into some hitherto unexplored part of the country, where there was a prospect of getting the adventures I wanted, together with a chance of making enough money to repair my misfortunes, seemed too good to be lost.

Arriving at Naivasha, I made a few inquiries, and found that I could get into the Kikuyu country by going north, crossing the Kinangop Plain, through the Masai country, and over the Aberdare Range—the highest peak of which is about 12,000 feet.

I thought that this would be the best point at which to enter the country, as, for one thing, it was the nearest to Naivasha, and if I was lucky enough to get the food, it would be easier to get it to the place where it was most needed.

CHAPTER IV

Government official tries to prevent me going into the Kikuyu country—Give the official the slip—My first acquaintance with the Kikuyu—Meet Karuri, the Kikuyu chief—Hospitable reception—Kikuyu village attacked because of my presence in it—I help to beat off the attack—Successful trading—Build a house in the Kikuyu village—Native theory as to the origin of the Kikuyu race—I help defend my Kikuyu friends from hostile raids, and beat off the enemy—Benefit of my conciliatory counsels—Pigasangi and blood brotherhood

HAVING made up my mind to go into the Kikuyu country, I set about preparing my safari, for which I decided to take with me only seven boys, natives who knew the language, to act as porters and carry the goods I was taking with me for trading with the Kikuyu. Having persuaded them that it would be all right, I armed myself with a rifle and fifty rounds of ammunition, and set out to explore the unknown.

When the official in charge of the station found that I had really started, he sent out an escort, under Sergeant Miles, to bring me back, and, of course, I had to go. When I got back to Naivasha, he asked me if I was trying to commit suicide. He said he dare not let me go, as I was certain to get killed, and he would then be held responsible for allowing me to leave his district. I told him that I would give him a written statement that I was going entirely on my own responsibility, and if I got killed it would not matter to him. His reply was that it was incumbent upon him not to allow me to leave his district. When I asked how far his district extended, he said to the Kedong Valley, about twenty miles from Naivasha.

I have before stated that the Government officials were strongly opposed to white men coming into the country, and Captain Gorges, who was in command at Naivasha, was only carrying out the orders of his superiors in trying to stop me. At this time there were only about ten white men who were independent traders and hunters in the whole of what are now the East African and Uganda Protectorates, besides the Government officials and missionaries—practically the whole of the latter class being up in Uganda. We were told plainly that we were not wanted, and were not even allowed to have guns and ammunition with which to protect ourselves; while the Arab and Swahili traders were allowed to overrun the country as they pleased, carrying and purchasing arms and ammunition as freely as they liked. This state of affairs *may* have been due to there being no organized administration in the country, off the caravan road; but it is peculiarly consistent with the Downing Street policy which prevails pretty well throughout our African dependencies, and which seems to be based on the principle that, in the eyes of Colonial Office officials, a native is more to be considered than any three white men.

To get beyond the jurisdiction of the official at Naivasha I went off to the Kedong Valley, which forms a portion of the great " rift " or depression which seems to divide the continent of Africa east from west into two portions, and which in those days was the boundary between British East Africa and Uganda. Naturally, I did not advertise my intention, but my determination was, as soon as I got out of his district, to start for the Kikuyu country, and by taking this step I avoided all further opposition and duly set out for my Land of Promise.

It was before the end of the year 1898 that, striking camp one morning, I entered the Kinangop Plain, a favourite grazing-ground of the Masai. The plain is a fine stretch of open country, rising in a gradual slope from the caravan road for about one thousand feet or more to the commencement of the bamboo forest,[1] which is known to the natives by the name of Menzini, "the place of bamboos." Owing to the elevation of this plain, rains are more frequent here, and when the lower lands are dry and parched, rich pasturage is to be found on the plain, while the ground is generally moist, and, on account of the lower temperature, its surface is often covered with a white rime in the mornings, and the air is cool and refreshing. The herds of sheep and cattle browsing suggest a country scene, such as is common in the Old Country.

As I was accompanied by two Masai boys, I met with no opposition from the warriors of that tribe camped on the plain to look after the safety of the herds; and during the first day's march we travelled about thirty miles, camping that night about eight thousand feet up the mountain-side, where we found the air very cold. Game was everywhere in abundance, and I also noticed a few elephant tracks; so the next morning we had a look round, and followed the elephant tracks, which we found went through the forest and over the mountain. We had great difficulty in forcing our way through the trackless bamboo forest. The bamboos grow as thick as wheat in a wheatfield, and even where the elephants had forced a way the trees they had broken were lying across their path. Bordering on the forest were steep

---

[1] The bamboo forests fringe the higher slopes of most of the mountains of East Africa, between the grass line and the windswept heights.

precipices, the depth of which was so great that objects in the valley below could only be very indistinctly seen. That night we ascended to a height of between eleven thousand and twelve thousand feet, and passing over the crest of the mountain, began the descent of the other side. Making a long day's trek, it was almost dark when we again camped for the night, still in the bamboo forest which covers the mountain-side.

So far we had met none of the Kikuyu people, and, continuing our march, we arrived, on the third day, in sight of the first native village. I had heard some one cutting wood in the forest off our road, and the news of our coming had spread. At the first sight of us the natives had started running away, but we soon heard the native war-cry being taken up from hill to hill round about, and could catch occasional glimpses of the natives themselves as they gathered in force towards the village. They were certainly a wild-looking lot, with their bodies smeared all over with grease and red clay, or, in some cases, a kind of whitewash, in which patterns were drawn according to the fancy of each individual, while fastened to the leg was a rattle, with an iron ball inside, which, as they moved about, made a noise very much like a railway train. Many of them wore wonderful head-dresses, made of the skin of the colobus monkey, and all were armed with spears and shields. These details I managed to notice as we were moving towards them.

In a short time quite five hundred warriors, fully armed, were drawn up outside the village, and, getting within speaking distance, I told my Masai interpreter to tell them that I had come to see the chief of the district.

Never having seen a white man before, they regarded me with something like awe, being evidently puzzled at my appearance, and were at a loss how to act. The fact that I had ventured to come there alone was, in itself, quite enough to surprise and astonish them, and, noting the impression I had made, I knew that if I was to succeed with them I must keep up an attitude of fearlessness.

After my interpreter had spoken, a guide came forward to conduct me to the chief, whose name was Karuri. Accompanying the guide to the chief's kraal, I was met by Karuri, who demanded to know what I wanted.

This important personage, who to-day collects the hut tax for the British Administration, would hardly be recognized as the savage warrior chief who now stepped forward to meet the first white man he had ever seen in his own country (as before explained, others had thought it more prudent to go round the outskirts). It was a strange meeting, and one which was to have great consequences for both of us. As time went on Karuri was to become my friend and right-hand supporter, while I, in turn, was to have an influence over him and his people which was to raise him to the position of a great chief and myself to supreme power in the country—a virtual King of the Kikuyu.

Through my interpreter, I explained as fully as possible my mission to his country, in answer to his inquiry. I said that I had come to see his country and was anxious to trade with him and to buy food. He then questioned me as to the force I had brought with me; to which I replied that, as my mission was a peaceable one, I had left most of my guns in the forest to avoid trouble, but that if he harmed me, my people would come and make war on him. This pardonable untruth seemed to make the desired impression on him, and he allowed me to give him a present of cloth, which he accepted with every appearance of pleasure. After this his manner became more friendly, and when I signified my intention of making a long stay in his country he readily agreed that his men should build a hut for me.

His people still regarded me suspiciously, but
obeyed my orders when I told them to fetch wood,
and set about the building of the hut, under my instructions. They also brought me a sheep and some
flour and sweet potatoes, and, as I had by this time
got a fire going, I had a good meal cooked for myself and my men, the Kikuyu all the time looking on
with much interest.

In the meanwhile I had been looking round and
taking stock of the neighbourhood, and a wilder
scene it would be hard to imagine. The Kikuyu
country is a succession of small hills, separated by
deep valleys, lined with water-courses fed from the
higher country, while the hills are beautifully wooded,
except where the trees have been cleared away to
get patches of ground for the cultivation of crops.

The village, which was situated on the high
ground in a large clearing in the forest, consisted
of a cluster of round huts, surrounded by a high thorn
fence, or boma, high enough and thick enough to
make any attempt at forcing an entrance by a
force unprovided with good axes a matter of great
difficulty. The entrance through the boma was by
means of a narrow tunnel, made of large slabs of
wood, sunk deeply in the ground, with the tops inter-
locking at such an angle that any one wishing to
enter had to crawl through it on hands and knees.
The walls of the huts were made of huge slabs of
wood, fashioned out of large trees by the simple process of cutting portions off the trunk until it was
reduced to the required thickness. These slabs were
placed upright in the ground, close together, in the
form of a circle, and a thatched roof built up over
them. By the side of the huts, which were built without any attempt at regularity, were smaller struc-
tures, with basket floors and grass roofs, which I
found were used as granaries, or larders, in which to
store the food.

The people who gathered round us while the

meal was being got ready were a fierce-looking crowd, their bodies being disfigured with paint and hung about with rough ornaments. Every one seemed to be discussing me, and, by the looks cast in my direction, debating whether, after all, they should not kill me. Not knowing what might happen, I kept my rifle near me and my bandolier in readiness in case of a sudden attack. After a time they became more inquisitive, and began to examine my clothes, which were something quite new to them, as they had never seen anything of the sort before. The boots puzzled them the most, as they appeared to think they were actually part of my feet, which they seemed to think very curiously constructed. Some of them pushed their curiosity to the extent of wanting to examine my rifle, but this I refused to let go out of my hand.

My interpreter said that they thought I was very foolish to come among them with only one rifle, so I told him to tell them that this gun was different from any that they had ever seen before and far more effective than those carried by Arab and Swahili traders. This gun, I explained, could kill six men with one shot, and I told them that I would show them what it would do by firing at a tree. It happened to be the old Martini-Metford, so, putting in a solid cartridge, I chose a tree that I knew the bullet would go through and fired. They immediately rushed in a body to see what damage had been done, and when they found the hole where the bullet had gone in and come out the other side they were both considerably surprised and impressed. I assured them that that was nothing; if they would examine the side of the mountain beyond they would find that the bullet had gone right through that as well! I knew that only sheer bluff could bring me safely out of the position in which I had voluntarily placed myself, and so made the best use of every opportunity that arose of impressing them.

Turning into my hut, I kept awake practically all
night, fearing that some treachery might be
attempted, but fell asleep at last, to be awakened
early in the morning by an awful row of warhorns
and men shouting and running about in every direction. By the time I had rubbed the sleep out of my
eyes I saw a crowd of very excited natives rushing in
a body towards my hut, and fully expected that I
was in for a tough fight. However, far from intending to attack me, they had come to implore my help
for themselves. It seemed that though Karuri, in his
younger days, had been a powerful chief, his influence
had waned as he grew older, and the tribe being split
up into clans, something like the Highlanders in the
old days, in the absence of a chief sufficiently strong
to keep the various sections in order, they were continually indulging in petty wars among themselves.
One of the neighbouring clans had heard of my
arrival, and, objecting to the presence of any white
man in the country, had promptly attacked Karuri's
village, with the object of disposing of me once for
all, and a big fight, in which a number of people had
already been killed, was then in progress, while, on
looking out of my hut, I saw that a portion of the
village was in flames.

My duty was clear. These people had brought the
trouble on themselves by befriending me, and the
least I could do was to give them such help as I
could. Besides, I wished to remain in the country,
and if these people were worsted—even if I escaped
with my life, which was very unlikely—I should have
to get out and stay out, for some considerable time,
at any rate. It did not take me long to make up my
mind, and, seizing my rifle, I made for the scene of
the fight, accompanied by a crowd of yelling savages,
delighted at my decision. When I arrived the row
was at its height and the sight of the hand-to-hand
conflict among the warriors, surrounded by the burning huts, was a stirring one. Seeing the reinforce-

ments, headed by myself, coming up, the attackers began to waver, and when I had fired a few shots with effect, finally turned tail and bolted. After pursuing them for some distance, to make sure that they were completely scattered, the triumphant warriors returned to the village, and made quite a hero of me, being convinced that their victory was entirely due to my help. This incident was of the greatest value to me, as it fully established my reputation as a useful member of the community, and they became very friendly. I learned that they had had a lot of trouble with this particular clan, who had frequently raided them, killing many of their men, and carrying off their cattle, and sometimes their women.

After this Karuri came to ask me if I would stop in his country, and I told him I would think about it. I said that I had other work to do, but that if he would sell me flour and other foodstuffs I would come back to him. I told him that the flour was for friends of mine, who were coming along the caravan road. He said that he did not want any more white people in the country. I could stop as long as I liked myself, and his people would be my friends, but they did not mean to have any strangers. I explained that though my friends were coming along the caravan road they had no intention or desire to enter the country. This explanation seemed to satisfy them, and I told them that I would not decide at once about staying in the country, but that when I had taken the flour to my friends I would come back and talk matters over with them. They then asked what I had to give in exchange for the flour, and I produced a bottle of iodoform, some of which I had used on their wounds after the fight with good effect. They thought it was a great medicine, and all wanted some, and in exchange for a small quantity, wrapped in paper, would give from ten to twenty pounds of flour.

They looked upon me as a great medicine man,

and members of the tribe came to me daily to be cured of various complaints during the fortnight I stayed with them while the food I wanted was being collected and brought in. When it was all in I found that I had about two hundred loads, and the trouble then was to find porters to carry it out of the country; but by dint of persuasion I finally succeeded in impressing a number of the people into my service, and started off with my loads.

On account of my little difference with Captain Gorges I decided not to go to Naivasha, but to carry my loads down towards the Kedong. As the route to the Kedong Valley led through the Masai country, my men would not go right through with it, so I set them to build a hut on the caravan road, where I established a store for the flour, and within a few days I sold the lot to the railway surveyors and caravans for about thirty rupees a load, which made me highly satisfied with the result of my first venture among the Kikuyu. It was on this journey that I first saw the native method of starting a fire by means of the " fire-stick," though subsequently I found it very useful on many occasions when, owing to the dampness during the rainy season, my matches would not light satisfactorily. The fire-stick itself is a piece of hard wood, about eighteen inches in length, of the thickness of a lead pencil and pointed, and is carried in the quiver with the arrows. The method of using it differs somewhat from that practised by certain tribes who are accustomed to use a sort of mandril in connexion with it. The Kikuyu always carry, as well as the fire-stick, a piece of wood of a softer kind, about a foot long and two or three inches wide, which, when they wish to make a fire, they place between their feet, holding it in position with their toes. The pointed fire-stick is inserted into a hole in the soft wood and rapidly revolved between the flat of their two hands until the dust worn off the softer wood by the friction begins to glow. This

burning dust is then quickly tossed into the middle of
a little bundle of dry bark fibre, always carried by
the owner of the drill.   The little bundle is then taken
between the hands and gently blown up until it
shows signs of blazing, when it is placed in the
middle of a little heap of dried twigs and leaves
which has been prepared in readiness.   A little careful manipulation soon produces a blaze.

I was also able to purchase a large quantity of
trade goods, beads, cloth, &c., from Arab traders
going up to Uganda, and sent to Karuri for more
natives to carry my purchases back to Kikuyu,
where, on my return, I paid them for their services
in cloth, which seemed to make them still more
anxious for me to remain among them.

Having finally announced my decision to stay in
the Kikuyu country, at any rate for a time, I selected
a site for a house, and got them to help me with the
building.   I found that they had a sort of native axe,
somewhat similar to those in use in the South Sea
Islands, made with a very small head, which is fixed
to the club which forms the haft by a spike projecting
from the back, which is driven through the haft and
projects for two or three inches at the back—and
with these and the swords, with which every man is
armed, they cut down trees from the forest, and a
house in the European style was built for me.

In connexion with these swords I may mention a
peculiar custom which illustrates the treacherous
nature of these people.   They invariably wear the
sword on the *right* side, as when worn in that position it is much easier to make a treacherous attack
on an opponent while approaching apparently with
the friendly intention of shaking hands!

Their method of tree-cutting was a somewhat dangerous one, as they simply cut into the tree near the
ground, without any regard to the direction in which
it was likely to fall, so that serious injuries during
tree-felling operations were by no means uncommon.

The Kikuyu never use nails, but by dint of careful explanation, I was able to get the native blacksmiths to make me a very efficient substitute.[1] The natives were very much interested in the building operations, and when the house was finished I used to invite the chief and his headmen to visit me there. The house, which was built in the bungalow style, common to European houses in the tropics, looked very well, and though the windows were, of course, unglazed, I had shutters made, with which I could close them at night.

In the meanwhile I had been getting better acquainted with the country, and found that the people lived in a constant state of civil war. Every day men came to me to have their wounds dressed, and I heard of many being killed. As I have already said, the country was very mountainous, and each hill had its own chief, who lived in a state of continual warfare with his neighbours. No man was safe in travelling about the country, except on certain days when a sort of general market was held, during the continuance of which a truce seemed to exist, hostilities being resumed again as soon as it was over. Karuri used to visit me nearly every day, and from him I learned all about the country. Even he seemed afraid to go far from his own village, and, as this state of affairs was very bad for my plans of trading, I determined to do what I could towards reducing the country to something like order.

I gathered, from conversations with Karuri and the older men of the village, that at one time the country was believed to have been covered with a vast forest, inhabited by a race of pigmies, whom they called Maswatch-wanya. These people did not cutivate the land, but lived by hunting, and the legend said that

---

[1] I have read that the use of nails was practically unknown in England until the latter half of the eighteenth century.

the wife of a Masai, who was very badly treated by
her husband, was in the habit of taking refuge in
the forest, with her little boy, from his cruelty. At
first she used merely to stay in the forest for a time,
and then return to her husband again; but at last his
treatment of her became so bad that she left him altogether, and took refuge with the pigmies, and it was
believed that the Kikuyu race were the descendants
of the offspring of this woman. There is certainly a
good deal of evidence to support the tradition, as they
undoubtedly have Masai blood, use the same kind
of weapons and shield, and in each case worship a
god they call Ngai. I have also heard them singing
Masai war-songs when going out to fight, and in a
very large number of instances the physical resemblance between the two races is very strong.

I stayed some weeks with them this time, and
found that there was a good deal of fighting going
on, and that many of the friendly natives were being
killed through the hostility to me of the neighbouring
chiefs and their people. They strongly resented my
intrusion into the country, and any of the natives
known to be friendly towards me, or wearing any of
the cloth I had given them, were immediately
marked down for attack.

This sort of thing went on for some time, and
they began to think that, because I took no action
against their enemies, I was afraid of them. There
were threats to kill me every day, and one night,
after some of their villages had been burned, and a
lot of the people killed, they came to me and asked me
to take their part, saying that they had always been
friendly towards me, and that was why these people
were making war on them and robbing them.

I therefore sent a messenger to the offending chief,
to say that if he did not return the stolen property,
and pay compensation for the murders he had committed, I should have to go and compel him to do
do so. (The law of the country is that for every man

killed a payment of one hundred sheep shall be made, and for every woman thirty sheep.) The chief simply returned an insulting message to the effect that we were afraid of him, and the next time he came he would kill me too.

A few days later I had a consultation with Karuri, and we came to the conclusion that the only thing to be done was to go out and fight the matter out with them, though I was strongly averse to getting mixed up in any of their quarrels. However, the matter was settled for us, for while we were still negotiating for a peaceful settlement of the difficulty, our enemies came down in force one day and attacked the village. They numbered altogether about five hundred warriors, while we could only muster about three hundred. They had been successful in previous raids because the people were scattered about in a number of small villages, and could not muster in sufficient force to beat them off, as they could always overwhelm a village and get away before any help could be brought to the spot. On this particular occasion, however, matters were a little different, as we had been expecting trouble, and had made arrangements to give them a warm reception if they should venture to come.

Our spies had been out for some time, and kept us well informed as to what was going on, and gave us good warning as to when we might expect to be attacked. As soon as the news of the approaching raid reached us, I mustered the fighting men and got ready to receive them. We were soon made aware of their approach by the sound of wild war-cries and savage yells, as well as by the flames of the burning villages, to which they set fire as they came along, and, meeting with no opposition, no doubt they anticipated an easy victory.

By this time I had taught my people to hold themselves in check, and act together, instead of each man fighting for his own hand. Waiting till they had got within easy striking distance, we poured in a volley of spears and arrows and I did service with my rifle. Following up the surprise caused by this unexpected reception, we were soon among them and engaged in a warm hand-to-hand fight, which lasted until we had beaten off the invaders and followed them right back into their own country. The battle, which had started in the early morning, lasted until midday, and, having administered severe punishment, we camped for the night in the enemy's district.

We had had the good fortune to capture the enemy's chief, who was brought a prisoner into our camp, and the next morning I consulted with Karuri as to what was to be done with him, and it was at last decided to hold a *shauri* (pronounced *showari*), or council, on the matter. I asked them what they would have done in a case like this if I had not been with them, and they replied that they would either have killed him or made him pay a heavy fine. I pointed out that killing him or making his people pay a heavy fine would only aggravate the enmity of these people, and so cause more trouble later on. I told them that it would be better to make the chief restore everything that had been stolen by him—not in previous years, but in the raids which had taken place during my stay among them, and to this course they finally agreed.

Within a few days all the stolen property was restored to its original owners, causing much rejoicing among them, as they had, of course, never expected to see any of it again. Of course, I took precautions to see that no friction occurred during the process of retransferring the recovered property, and having invited some of the chief men of both districts to my camp, we got on quite friendly terms. Seeing them sitting, eating and drinking together amicably, it was difficult to imagine that they had been cutting one another's throats only a few days previously, but the Kikuyu, like many other African races, are remarkably changeable, and their temper can never be relied upon. As I learnt during my stay among them, they are both fickle and treacherous, and had it not been for my own people, I should have run great risk of being killed on several occasions, through trusting them too much.

I was very anxious to strengthen and maintain my friendship with these people and the surrounding clans, and, after some discussion on the matter, found that they had a ceremony, known as Pigasangi, which was supposed to be mutually binding. If it could be arranged for me to undergo this ceremony, there was every prospect of a lasting friendship being formed. This ceremony differs from that of blood-brotherhood chiefly in that, while blood-brotherhood establishes a friendly relationship with the individual, Pigasangi establishes it with the whole of the tribe or communities represented at the ceremony.

After some days the assembled chiefs consented to take part in the ceremony, and, accompanied by the natives who had always been friendly to me, and about fifteen of the old men of the district, I went to the chief's village to make the necessary arrangements.

When we arrived at the village the people were already waiting to receive us, and there were signs of great festivity. Word had been sent round to all the villages that the ceremony was to take place, and, as it was looked upon as a great occasion for rejoicing, much dancing and beer-drinking were going on, and we were received with shouts of welcome and every sign of friendship. A large clearing had been selected for the occasion—the Kikuyu, like many other savage tribes, always choosing an open space for their ceremonies, or discussions of importance, as they were thus enabled to detect any would-be eavesdroppers before they could get near enough to overhear anything or to attempt any treachery. Nearly all native villages, I found, have a large space set apart in the neighbourhood for the holding of their shauris, dances, &c.

After a lot of superfluous oratory, the proceedings began with a black goat being brought in, with its feet tied up, and laid in the centre of the space. The natives then grouped themselves in a circle, with the chiefs and orators in the centre. Everybody taking part in the ceremony had previously disarmed, and, considering that there were over two thousand people present, it was remarkable how orderly and quiet the assembly was, everything being carried out without any hustling or disputing for right of place.

The native never speaks at any meeting of the tribe without a stick in his hand, and on the present occasion each speaker was provided with a number of sticks, having one for each subject of discussion, the sticks being thrown on the ground by each alternately as he went through his speech. First one side and then the other stated the points of the agreement, which, of course, had been carefully discussed beforehand, so that there should be no chance of argument during the ceremony. The main points were that there were to be no hostilities between the two clans in future, that they were to assist each other, and that neither should molest any white man coming through its country.

When all the sticks had been thrown down, they were collected, and being bound up in a bundle, were placed between the legs of the goat. The chief orator, whose stick was more like a club than the rest, then repeated the different conditions, at the end of each clause dealing the goat a heavy blow with his club whilst repeating a formula to the effect that any one breaking the agreement should die like that goat. By the time he had reached the last clause the animal was almost dead, and a particularly heavy blow dispatched it. After that no one dare touch the goat, which was regarded as sacred, and I learned that this was the opportunity to obtain any confession from a native, any one suspected of wrongdoing being asked to swear by the goat, when he would certainly tell the truth.

The ceremony was followed by more rejoicing and drinking of native beer.

This function considerably enlarged the area of friendly country, which now extended to the banks of one of the rivers which rises in the Aberdare Range, and flows in an easterly direction until it empties, as I afterwards found, into the River Tana.

On the other hand, the fact of these people making friends with me had the effect of increasing the enmity of the other chiefs, who remained outside the agreement, and feared that the effect of it would be to lead more white men to come into the country.

CHAPTER V

Am established in the country—Native festivities and dances—Troubadours—Musical quickness of the natives—Dearth of musical instruments—My attempts at military organization—Hostile rumours—Preparations for resisting attack—Great battle and defeat of the attacking tribes—Victory due to skilful tactics of my Kikuyu force—Succeed in taking a large convoy of provisions into the starving Government stations—White men attacked and killed—Am supreme in the tribe—Native poisons—AlthoughI am supplying the Government stations with food, I get no recognition at the hands of the officials

THE people in the immediate neighbourhood of the district where I was living now looked upon me as a great man. My advice had been good in their councils, and I had succeeded in bringing about peace with their bitterest enemies. They also regarded me as a great medicine man, on the strength of the iodoform, and of a bottle of Eno's fruit salts, which they would come round in crowds to watch me drink, saying that the white man could drink boiling water; and they believed that I must have a stomach like iron, and, being utterly ignorant, my friends were firmly convinced that it was impossible to kill me.

The news of my presence spread all through the country, and many threats to kill me were uttered —it being reported that some of the hostile chiefs were banding together for that purpose.

In the meanwhile, I invited some of the principal

witch doctors to come and live near me, and at intervals of about ten days I would get the natives round
about to come up to my house to dance. These
dances were always held during the daytime, and
the women took no part in them. The Kikuyu are
a very musical people, singing wherever they go,
and the warriors would come to the dances in a
body, singing as they marched along, and keeping
as perfect time and step as a regiment of trained
soldiers. First of all they would have a kind of
march past, and then, falling out, would form a
huge circle, with all the women and the old men on
the outside. First one warrior and then another
would dart out from the circle and go through
some weird evolutions. Every man was fully armed
as if going on the war-path, and the movements took
the form of a fierce fight with an imaginary enemy,
each man, as he jumped out of the circle, rushing
round and spearing his imaginary foe. If the man
was recognized as a great warrior, he was violently
applauded by the onlookers, and, encouraged by the
signs of approbation, would work himself up into a
perfect frenzy; but if he was a man who had not
distinguished himself in any way, or who was not
popular among the tribesmen, his performance would
be received in absolute silence.

One peculiar point that struck me about these
people was the absence of any kind of musical instrument, even the usual drum. All their songs and
dances were absolutely unaccompanied by any of the
usual weird noises that, with most savage tribes,
represent a musical accompaniment, and the only
musical instrument that I ever knew of their making
was a kind of whistle, something after the fashion
of those made by boys at home from elder stems, and,
I imagine, merely a toy; certainly I never saw them
used by any but boys, and only on rare occasions by
the boys themselves. I do not include among musical
instruments the war-horn, an instrument usually

made from the horn of a bullock or the koodoo, and which is used simply as an alarm.

One peculiar point about the applause on these occasions was that it was confined to the women, the men considering it beneath their dignity to make any demonstration, whether of approval or contempt. Although the women were not allowed to take any part in these dances themselves, they always appeared in full force as spectators, rigged out in their best go-to-meeting suits of skins, with their bodies plentifully smeared with grease, and wearing all their ornaments. When any favourite warrior had the floor, they expressed their approval by waving bunches of grass, and at the same time raising a musical chant of " lu-lu-lu-lu-lu." This chant, by the way, was the common form of welcome among them, as, when my safaris returned from one of my trips to Naivasha with food, the women would all turn out as we approached a village and greet us with this cry, which was taken up from hill to hill as we went along.

They had some dances in which the women joined, and these were usually held at night round a big fire. The Kikuyu seem to have more varieties of dances than any natives I know, and are, on the whole, a light-hearted race, singing all day long.

They have a class of strolling minstrels, resembling more than anything the old troubadours of the Middle Ages. There were only five or six of these troupes in the country altogether, and, like the troubadours, they were a privileged class, travelling from place to place and extemporising songs about local events and people—not always without a strong tinge of sarcasm, which no one dared to resent.

The Kikuyu were particularly clever in picking up the songs introduced by these troubadours, and a song that took the popular fancy would be taken up at its first hearing, and spread through the country with as much, or even more rapidity than a music-hall ditty among the errand-boys of London, dis-appearing as rapidly when a new one came out.

There was a further resemblance to the trouba-dours in the fact that they dressed in a fashion of their own, and wore a ring of small bells strapped round each ankle, and a single large one of iron fastened to each knee. They seemed to be free to pass where they pleased throughout the country, and I consequently encouraged them to visit me—which some of them would do every week—as they were able to keep me informed as to what was going on all over the country, so that I was able to meet any emergency that might arise.

The dances I arranged as a means of bringing the people together, so that I could talk to them after-wards and explain various things to them which they did not at first understand, such as the coming of the white men, who, I explained, did not come to raid their villages and make slaves of them, but wished to be friends in trade with them.

The information I got from some of my visitors with regard to what was going on in the outlying districts was also very useful at times. For instance, about this time I found that a tribe whose district lay to the north of us was preparing to make a big raid through the whole country, as they did not want any white men there at all; and I also got news from time to time of Arab and Swahili traders being murdered on their way down from the north from the Turkana country.[1]

Of course, these things put me on my guard, and I began to get the men together and to give them some little military training, so that we might be ready for any attack that should come. One point in particular that gave me a lot of trouble was teach-ing them to keep guard. It is a peculiarity of the

---

[1] The Turkana country lies to the west of Lake Rudolph.

African native that even when surrounded by the
enemy and expecting attack at any minute, he has
no idea of keeping on the alert and watching for
his foe. I had a remarkable instance of this in the
case of my own servant, a Swahili, whom I found
herding sheep for the Kikuyu, and took into my service. He had originally come to the country with
a caravan of Swahili traders, who, with the exception
of himself, had all been murdered. I put him among
my askaris (soldiers), and one night when he was
on guard, on making my usual round to see that all
was right, I found him lying on the ground fast
asleep at his post. I took his rifle away, and as that
did not wake him I poured a bucket of water over
his head. Even that did not disturb him much, the
only effect being to make him shiver and pull his
coat over his head—possibly thinking it was raining
—and then go on sleeping as peacefully as ever.
So I called the other men and pointed him out to
them, and they slipped a noose round his legs and
pulled him by his feet, while I fired a shot in the air
over his head. I thought that this would give him
such a fright that he would never go to sleep on
guard again, but it did not work and I had to find
him another job. It might have been thought that
his experience of having all his companions murdered
through not keeping a proper guard would have been
sufficient to make him keep awake, but this care-
lessness of such dangers is a native peculiarity which
is very hard to overcome.

As I have said, I found it very necessary to have
the natives better organized, from a military point
of view, seeing the danger with which we were
threatened, not only in respect of keeping guard, but
also in their method of fighting. They had never
been accustomed to observe any sort of formation in
their attack, but simply made a mad rush at the
enemy, so I taught them to keep together, forming
a line with their shields touching. I had one or two

lines in front of men armed with spears and shields, while the bowmen, with their poisoned arrows, took their place behind, protected by the shields of those in front. I had very few rifles, but hearing that there were some in the country—a good way farther north—which had been taken from some Swahili traders who had been murdered, I made a night march to secure them, and succeeded in collecting about one hundred, but only some thirty of them were of any real use. Having managed to get some ammunition, I selected the best men out of the tribe and armed them with these rifles, taking great trouble in teaching them how to use them. After a time I was able to put the squad through the manual exercises in English, though it always puzzled me to know how they understood what I wanted them to do, as not one of them knew a word of English, but I suppose they simply imitated what they saw me do when showing them the various movements, and associated certain sounds with those movements.

All this time the country was in a terrible state of unrest. Every night alarming messages were brought in that the people from the north were coming down to attack us. One night it would be the followers of Wagombi—a big chief living near Mount Kenia, who could muster two or three thousand fighting men—who were on the war-path. This chief had raided the whole of the country at one time or another, and, though I had tried to get messengers through to him in the hope of making friends with him, they were always murdered. Another night it would be the people of Tato who were coming down on us. All this time food was being collected and brought in, and I was anxious to explore the country still further, but was afraid to leave, on account of these rumours of threatened attacks. If I had gone away I should have had to take the best of the people with me, and I knew that during my absence the hostile tribes would have come down on the district, burnt the place out, and killed every one that was left. Besides, all the people urged me to stay with them, and not to go away just yet.

I had taken the precaution of placing outposts to give us due warning of any attack, which I expected would take place, if it did come, early in the morning, just before daylight, this being the usual time for an attack, and for this reason the Kikuyu will not keep fowls lest the crowing of the cocks towards dawn should betray their villages—which are always hidden away in the bush—to the enemy. This practice of delivering their attack just before dawn prevails among savage tribes pretty well all over the world, and I think that the chief reasons which lead to this time being chosen are, firstly, that the night offers the best opportunity of gradually bringing the force up into such a position that the enemy are surrounded before they can discover the movement which is in progress, and, secondly, that it is the hour at which vitality is at the lowest point, and consequently, the desire for rest and sleep has greater power over the body, and the force attacked is likely to be less alert and less fitted for strenuous resistance.

One night an attack was actually made on us, though it did not turn out to be anything very serious, and was possibly simply a piece of bravado on the part of some of the young warriors who were anxious for war. They had not time to do much damage before we arrived on the scene and repulsed them, with the loss of a few killed.

Up to this time I had not really attached much importance to the rumours that an attack was to be made on us from that quarter, though I had taken all precautions against being caught napping; but this put me more on the alert than ever, while my people were absolutely terrified—especially as the

latest rumour said that the people of Tato, who were
coming down on us, had got the Masai to join
them, as well as many of the Kikuyu who lived on
the other side of the river which, as I explained
before, was the boundary of the friendly district.
This river was nearly two days' march from the
farther boundary of the Kikuyu country, and the inhabitants of the intervening district had made friends
with the Masai to save themselves from being raided
—indeed, those on the boundary were half Masai
themselves, having largely inter-married with that
tribe. They would probably be able to muster a
force of about two thousand fighting men; so having
come to the conclusion that there was something in
the rumour—after having made inquiries and carefully thought the matter out—I saw that it was
necessary that we should be thoroughly prepared,
and set to work to make my plans accordingly.
Crossing the country through which the enemy would
have to come was a deep ravine, with a river
running through it. This river was crossed by a few
bridges consisting simply of felled trees, which had
been cut down so as to fall across the stream. I gave
orders to destroy or remove these bridges at once,
with the exception of one, against which I kept
a guard night and day, to give us full warning of
the enemy's coming; my intention was to destroy the
bridge as soon as the opposing force had crossed
it, in the hope that I might be able to teach them
such a lesson that they would leave us alone for the
future.

At the top of the mountain overlooking the ravine
I had built another house for myself, with a food
station and trading store attached—as I made use
of every opportunity of trading—and it was here that
I decided to wait for the invaders. I had put a guard
there, which I visited every day myself, to see that
things were all in order. The only path up the hill
from the bridge over the river zig-zagged up the

mountain-side, and was very rough and steep, so that it was difficult for an enemy to approach in a body.

The people living near this station were in continual fear of an attack, as they had news from their spies that a considerable number of Masai were on the Kikuyu boundary, near Tato, and it had been the custom of this tribe to raid the country at least once a year, when the young braves would come out on the war-path after the circumcision ceremony to prove their fighting qualities. Their main object was loot, but they did not hesitate to kill all who opposed them, besides burning the villages and carrying off the cattle—and very often the women as well. I determined if possible to put an end to this raiding and wanton bloodshed.

The men guarding the bridge had been instructed to send two of their number to bring me word as soon as they saw the enemy approaching, while the remainder were to stay behind in hiding, and destroy the bridge as soon as the invaders had crossed, so as to cut off their retreat. The long-expected attack came early one morning, and, following out their instructions, the watchers at the bridge gave me early warning that a large body of warriors had crossed the river, and we were quite ready to give them a warm reception. They came boldly on, never thinking that we were waiting for them, and no doubt expecting the same easy victory that they had had on previous raids. But a big surprise was in store for them. Owing to the narrowness of the path, they could only approach in single file, and we waited until they had almost reached the top before letting them know we were there. I had given strict orders that no man was to make a move, or utter a sound, until I gave the signal by firing my rifle. Coming steadily on, they had got close upon us when I fired, and my rifle-men opened on them at once, while the bowmen followed the volley up with a flight of

poisoned arrows. The invaders were taken completely by surprise, and before they could recover
themselves the Kikuyu warriors swept down on them
with swords and spears. Bolting in a mad panic,
they were hotly pursued down the mountain-side,
suffering severely in their flight. Arriving at the
river, they found that the bridge was gone, and many
of them jumped into the stream, of whom some got
safely across, but a good many were drowned on the
way. At least fifty had been killed, and many
wounded, and these I gave orders were not to be
killed, but brought in as prisoners, of whom, when
all were collected, we had a very large number, so
that the victory was altogether complete, while my
force had suffered only very slight loss. The punishment we had administered was so severe that the
country was never again raided by these people during
the time I was with the Kikuyu.

This victory having ensured the people security from
any further raids—for a time, at any rate—I had now
the opportunity for which I had been looking, of
taking the food I had collected into the British settlement. I had bought a lot of flour, which I took into
the Government station at Naivasha, and very pleased
they were to get it, as I found that they were practically starving for want of food. Not only was this
the case at Naivasha, but they were no better off at
the Ravine; and so thankful were the Government to
get these supplies that they made a contract with me
to keep them provisioned, and I heard no more about
my going into the Kikuyu country without permission !

It was on this visit to Naivasha that I was able
to renew my acquaintance with two most interesting
people, whom I had met on some of my journeys with
food for the troops in Uganda. They were Mr. and
Mrs. Walsh, who, at the time I first met them, were
engaged, like myself, in taking up food in donkey-
wagons for the troops. They had, I found, estab-

lished the first store in Naivasha. This was what I had wished to do some time previously, but had been forbidden by the official in charge—who, as I now have reason to believe, far exceeded his legal powers in doing so; but I was only a settler, and he was one of the officials who had his knife into me.

This couple had come to East Africa from Mashonaland, where Mrs. Walsh had been the first white woman to enter the country, and had started by taking up the transport business, in which they had both had considerable experience, and in which Mrs. Walsh took a man's share of the work, being the only white woman who ever ran transport in British East Africa. In spite of their many successful ventures, they are not numbered among the wealthy, their open-handed hospitality and careless, happy-go-lucky Irish temperament being against them in the race to accumulate riches; but there is hardly any one who has been in British East Africa who does not know them, and few who have not, at one time or another, shared their generous hospitality, which was as freely extended to the trader or settler temporarily down on his luck as to the Government official or missionary travelling in luxury.

I gave the authorities a full report on the country, telling them of the continual fighting and the trouble I had had right through. They said that they were quite aware of it, and that I could expect nothing else, but that they could give me no assistance, as they had quite enough troubles of their own, with the natives near at hand.

It appeared that during my absence from the Kikuyu country my old partner Gibbons had returned from Uganda and gone into partnership with a man named Findlay to make a trading expedition to the Kikuyu country; but I had somehow missed him while transacting my business in Naivasha, as his route had lain farther to the east. I found that as soon as the two had entered the country they had had

trouble with the natives, and some of their men had
been killed. They had taken with them forty or
fifty men, armed with rifles, and about one hundred
porters, intending to trade for ivory. So far as I
could gather, a chief had come to them and told
them that he had a tusk to sell. When the Kikuyu
come to sell ivory they do not show you the tusk but
give you the measurement, from which you have to
guess the weight; then, after the bargain is struck,
you pay for the ivory, and the seller is supposed to
bring it in. Gibbons bought a tusk, and sent ten
armed men back with the chief to bring it in.
These men were Swahili, who were terribly
afraid of the Kikuyu. They had received the
ivory, and were bringing it back to camp, when they
were all ambushed and murdered. The rest of the
safari lost heart at the murder of their companions
and had scarcely courage to defend themselves, and
Gibbons saw that his only chance was to build a boma,
as the natives were coming in force to attack him.
They had barely completed the boma when they were
attacked, and throughout the night the improvised
fort was surrounded by a yelling horde of savages,
bombarding them with spears and arrows and trying
by every means to get through the defences. Gibbons
and Findlay kept up a plucky defence, and by spur-
ring on their men managed to beat off the attack.
Things, however, looked even worse in the morning,
when the natives were reinforced, and hemmed them
in on every side. It was impossible to remain in the
boma, as they could not hope to hold it for long
against the hundreds of black fiends who surrounded
them, and it was decided to make a sortie and, if
possible, cut their way through and get out of the
country. The attempt was made, and a fierce hand-
to-hand fight ensued, in which Findlay received two
bad spear thrusts, and would have been killed out-
right had not one of his boys come to the rescue,
firing his rifle so close to Findlay's assailant that he

blew his arm clean off. Findlay was carried back into the boma, to which Gibbons and the few survivors also returned, and managed to strengthen their defences sufficiently to enable them to hold the savages at bay until a messenger could get through to the nearest Government station, from which a relief force of the King's African Rifles was sent out, and after a week of terrible hardship Gibbons and his few remaining followers were rescued. Findlay however, died later of his wounds.

This incident gives a good idea of the treacherous and bloodthirsty nature of the people among whom I was now spending my life.

On returning to Karuri's I found myself on better terms than ever with the natives, and many other chiefs came in to profess their friendship. By this time I could speak Swahili well, and had mastered the Kikuyu language sufficiently to understand what they were saying, although I still spoke to them through an interpreter, as I thus had time to consider my replies. My thorough defeat of their sworn enemies, the Masai, had given me a great reputation among them, which was increased by their belief that it was impossible to kill me, a belief which had been strengthened by my defying the witch doctors to poison me and swallowing, in their presence, samples of what they considered their most deadly poisons without any ill effects. In consequence of the reputation I had thus gained my word was law, and I advised them that it would be greatly to their advantage to stop quarrelling and fighting among themselves, which advice I backed by severely punishing any one I caught quarrelling. With regard to my singular immunity from the effects of the poisons of the native witch doctors, it is, perhaps, difficult to find a satisfactory explanation. Whenever I met a witch doctor I always insisted on sampling any poisons he might have with him, which were always prepared with honey, and appeared to me to be a mixture of honey and the ashes of burnt herbs—a black, sticky mess—and though not, perhaps, the most appetising morsel one could choose, yet not so unpleasant to the taste as to be objectionable. But, in spite of the opportunities thus offered them to get rid of the one man in the country whom they both hated and feared, I never felt the slightest ill-effects from these experiments. On the other hand, it must not be supposed that I ordinarily took any undue risks of death by poison. I never accepted any drink offered by my savage acquaintances or hosts without first seeing that the person who brought it carried out the usual custom of sampling it himself before I touched it, while I took all necessary precautions to ensure that my food was not interfered with.

Several theories occur to my mind to account for my immunity. One is that the concoctions which I took, in spite of the witch doctors' assurances that they were deadly, were not poisons at all. I think it quite likely that they never carried their real poisons on them, but specially prepared them, in the secrecy of their own huts, for each individual, and that they were merely trying to frighten me.[1]

Another is that the Kikuyu had no poisons at all.[2] It must be remembered that the African native is one of the most superstitious beings in the world, and there is no doubt that many of the deaths attributed to the action of the witch doctors were really due to pure funk. The natives are so oppressed with a belief in the occult powers of the medicine man that it is well known that it is generally quite sufficient for him to curse an individual and assure him that his

---

[1] It is the Wakamba who deal in poisons and sell them to the neighbouring tribes. They pretend to have a monopoly of them in East Africa.

[2] The poison put on their arrows is, I believe, innocuous if merely swallowed; it needs to be inoculated in the blood to be effective.

death will take place on or before a certain time to ensure that the man will simply give up the ghost according to the prophecy. Instances of this sort of thing can be quoted in connexion with most primitive races, either in Africa or India. I know very well that some of the native races of British East Africa have deadly poisons, and do not hesitate to use them, as two white men of my acquaintance met with horrible deaths from poison administered by some Wakamba, while I know of more than one similar instance occurring among white men on the West Coast. But with the native the ingrained superstitious fear of the medicine man is generally quite sufficient to cause death under the influence of his curse. So deeply rooted in the native mind is this belief in the power of these quacks that I know of a native doctor, holding the post of Assistant Colonial Medical Officer in one of our West Coast colonies, who definitely stated that he could do nothing for a certain man who was ill, and of whom it was rumoured among the natives that he had trodden on poison which had been scattered on the floor of his house by a native medicine man for the purpose of poisoning him. This official was a prominent member of the Church of England in the colony and the possessor of several first-class European qualifications, yet he frankly said that he could do nothing against the arts of his heathen rival!

It is quite possible that a reason for my escape may be found in the superstitious fears of the witch doctors themselves. One of the greatest assets of these men was the belief, which they carefully fostered among the natives, that any one attempting to injure them would bring some terrible disaster upon himself. If they actually believed this themselves—and by constant reiteration of the fraud they may at last have brought themselves to believe it to be a truth—it is quite likely that they feared that any attempt to injure me, whom they reluctantly admitted to be more powerful than themselves, would, in the same way, recoil on their own heads.

I may mention that the medicine men of the Fantee and Ju-Ju systems, on the West Coast, frankly admit that their arts are of no use against the white man, who absolutely disbelieves in them, so that possibly my want of faith in their mummery served to protect me from their kindly attentions and from any serious attempts at poisoning.

It should be remembered also that by " medicine " is meant incantation—that the drug is supposed to act rather through the medium of the incantation than through any potency of its own. Hence the powers of a poison to do harm would depend more on the magic possessed by the medicine man than on the power of the drug. So that a poison would have no power to injure a medicine man possessed of more magic than the man administering the drug.

After collecting more food, I went down with it again to the Government station at Naivasha, the road to which, through the bamboo forest, was extremely difficult; but when I wanted to improve the track the Kikuyu strongly objected, saying that if a road were made it would make it much easier for the Masai to raid them. As it was, in case of a raid, they could get away with their cattle through the bamboo forest. But if roads were made through the forest they would be at the mercy of the raiders. They also feared a descent by the Kalyera, another branch of the Kikuyu tribe, along the fringe of whose country I had to pass when taking supplies down to Naivasha. Where their path joined the main road into the Masai country my caravans were frequently waylaid. To put a stop to this I built a camp at the junction of the two paths, and left some armed men in charge, but they were continually being attacked, and several of them were killed.

On getting the food into Naivasha I was told that there was no limit to the quantity they would take if I could only provide it. I again made a report to the Government as to the difficulty I had in obtaining the supplies; but, as usual no notice was taken.

CHAPTER VI

I determine to extend my operations into more remote districts of the Kikuyu country—New friends—Native taste for tea—Plague of ants—Curious superstition with regard to milking cows—The Kalyera reject my friendly overtures—Trouble at headquarters—Tragic interview with a recalcitrant chief—Gain further prestige thereby—Further plans—Take my Kikuyu followers down to Mombasa—Their impressions in contact with civilization

ON returning to my home among the Kikuyu I found that the country was fairly quiet, so I thought I would take the opportunity to explore a little farther into the interior, and, if possible, make friends among some of the other chiefs, thus enlarging the area from which I could draw supplies of food. My idea was to build trading stations at various points in the country, and, leaving a few men in charge at headquarters, to organize a fairly large expedition to explore other parts of the country and induce the natives to make friends and trade with me.

The first people I wished to come to terms with were the Kalyera, who had given me so much trouble on the road to Naivasha. I wished to prevent my people being killed when taking the food down, and as these murders had been on the increase, I was afraid that they would eventually block the road. I determined to keep the route open at all costs, it being the only way into Naivasha. As I have already said, the Kikuyu country is very hilly and difficult for travelling, and to reach Kalyera we should have to cross several mountains and rivers.

Having prepared my expedition, we set off. All the country through which we passed was under cultivation, by which I mean that wherever a clearing had been made in the forest the land was either growing food or had been abandoned in fallow after being under cultivation for some time; the custom of the Kikuyu being to cultivate the land until it showed signs of becoming exhausted and then make a fresh clearing and repeat the process.

The first day passed without any trouble at all from the natives, who were all more or less friendly towards me in this part, and our first camp was pitched in the territory of a typical native chief, a rather stout and quite jolly sort of fellow, who owned a large number of cattle, sheep, and goats, and who seemed a good deal more like a Masai than a Kikuyu. I had not seen him before, but he had sent some of his people to help me against the hostile tribes who had come down to attack us. He wanted me to stay there altogether, but I told him that my headquarters were at Karuri's, and then delighted his heart with a present of a blanket and fez, which pleased him immensely. His people called me Karanjai, meaning literally " Who eats beans," because I preferred that vegetable to their sweet potatoes. In connection with this nickname of Karanjai several amusing incidents occurred before I found out what was actually meant by it. Names of this sort, which the natives are very clever in bestowing, once given, rapidly become known throughout the country, so that it was nothing unusual for me to be greeted as Karanjai on my first visit to some village in a part of the country quite new to me, and it was, therefore, not unnatural that I should think it was some form of greeting, and for a long time, when any native addressed me as Karanjai, I replied by repeating the word, thinking that I was thus com-

plying with native etiquette. It was the more difficult for me to get at the real meaning as my own
people would give me no satisfactory explanation,
fearing that I should be annoyed if I found that
they had given me a nickname. When I did finally
discover what it meant, it was impossible to be annoyed, as there was nothing objectionable in the
name itself, and I could not help admitting that it
was peculiarly appropriate.

As time went on, and my power and influence in
the country extended, it was quite usual, when I
visited a village, for several proud fathers to bring
small sons to be introduced to me, explaining that
they also had been named Karanjai in my honour.

They had never seen a white man before, and
likened me to their god Ngai, as I was a great
medicine man, and they believed that I could make
rain. They also thought that I was unkillable, but,
knowing their treacherous nature, I never allowed
myself to be caught off my guard. The Kikuyu
will come up to you smiling and kill you the next
moment if he gets the chance. This happened in
the case of a man who went out to buy food only
about twenty miles from Fort Smith. The chief
came up to him smiling, and while he shook hands
with one hand drew his sword with the other, and
the man barely escaped with his life, while all the
men with him were killed. As before stated, they
wear their swords on the right side, as the action
of drawing the sword is less noticeable from that
side, and their opponent has less warning of their
intention.

This chief, Wunjaggi, had been notified of my
coming by a messenger sent on ahead of the party,
and sent out some of his warriors to welcome me,
who plucked handfuls of grass and waved them as
a sign of peace. The chief met me with a huge
spear in his hand, which, as soon as he saw me,
he stuck in the ground, and we then shook hands in

the native fashion, first spitting in our palms. I had discouraged this practice of hand-shaking among my own people, and taught them to make a military salute instead, as a precaution against treachery. He seemed very pleased to see me, and told me that he had heard a lot about the white man. As we entered the village his people began singing, and my followers joined in, and there was general jubilation.

The chief gave me a present of sheep for myself and my men, and when we had selected a site and pitched out tent some njohi[1] was sent in, which I gave orders to be taken to my own tent and gave out to the men myself, as I knew that when they got too much they were not responsible for their actions, and would be sure to cause trouble. During the day quite a lot of people came to see me, as they had never seen a white man before, so I had a strong guard posted round the camp, only allowing a few natives to come in at a time, and all had to disarm before entering the camp. Of course, everything I had of European make was quite new to them, even to the tent; but they seemed most particularly interested in the knives and forks, while the enamelled cups and saucers and plates also excited their curiosity. Everything I did seemed to them making magic. If I happened to be reading a paper, they thought I was doing so for some occult purpose, and when I smiled at a funny paragraph they watched me curiously, and all began to laugh too, although they had not the faintest idea what I was amused at.

I invited the chief to drink tea with me, out of a cup and saucer, and at first he took a lot of persuading, but after tasting the tea he liked it so much that I had reason to regret having introduced the practice, as both he and the various other chiefs I met got so fond of it that they would demand it

---

[1] A native drink.

whenever they saw me. They were also very fond of salt, which they would eat by the handful. This fondness for salt may seem to those who are accustomed to use it without stint, and even waste large quantities carelessly, rather peculiar; but it must be borne in mind that in many parts of the world besides the Kikuyu country salt is a very rare article and a heavily-taxed luxury, every grain of which must be carefully economised. The Kikuyu obtained the requisite salt for their animals from certain salt-pans, or, as they are called in some parts of the world, salt-licks, which were places where the earth was sufficiently mixed with saline particles to give it a fairly strong, brackish taste. This earth is dug up by the natives and mixed with water till it is of the consistency of liquid mud; it is then placed in the cattle-troughs, and it is a strange sight to see the animals devouring this muddy mess with every appearance of enjoyment. For their own use they used to burn large quantities of green papyrus reed, mixing the ashes with their food instead of salt. This plant, although it grows in the fresh-water lakes and streams, contains a fair proportion of saline matter, so that the ashes form a substitute—though, to my taste, a very inefficient one—for salt.

As the country here was about seven thousand feet above sea-level it became very cold at night, and I had always a big fire lighted at sundown, and before turning in saw that a good guard was set.

During our first night among my new friends, we had a most unpleasant experience, in the shape of a visitation from an army of brown ants, which came right through the camp. These brutes—they are about half an inch long, and so may be rightly called brutes—have very powerful jaws, like the claws of a lobster, and bite most fearfully. They covered everything in their path, and, getting into the blankets, drove me out of my tent, and caused every one to dance about in the most comical fashion in their efforts to get rid of the pests. So tenacious were they that one could hardly pull them off, and the whole camp was in an uproar during the hours that the army took to pass, and there was little more sleep that night for any one. I do not know to what particular variety of the ant tribe these brutes belonged, but I should think that they must bear a strong resemblance to the kind known as " the bull-dog ant," which is, among certain African tribes, looked upon as a valuable assistant to the native surgeon, who uses it instead of the silk thread and surgical needle of civilization for sewing up wounds. The manner in which they are used for this purpose is as follows : The edges of the wound are drawn together, and held in that position with the fingers of the left hand, while with the right a bull-dog ant is picked up and held so that the jaws grip one on each side of the wound; the body of the ant is then twisted off, while the head still remains, tenaciously holding on to the flesh. From this habit of holding on they have acquired the name of bull-dog. The Kikuyu did not make any such use of these ants, though their method of sewing up wounds was scarcely less primitive. In their case the edges of the wound were drawn together and a long thorn run through both. A fine thread, made of fibre from the bark of certain trees, is then wound over both ends of the thorn, in the same way that sailors wind the spare ends of ropes round the cleats. The thorn is left in place till the wound heals, and then drawn out in the same way that a surgeon removes the stitches after more civilized operations.

Next morning we struck camp and umed our journey, the chief accompanying me to the boundary of his territory. On the way he told me that he had had a lot of trouble with the neighbouring tribes, particularly the people I was going to visit, the Kalyera, with whom he was in a state of continual warfare. He parted from me with a serious warning to be very careful, as the people I should next meet were very treacherous.

We had started about 6 p.m., and about five hours' march brought us to the village of the next chief named Caranja, whose looks I did not like from the first, as he had a most truculent and treacherous appearance, so that, although he shook hands with me readily when we met, I did not trust him, and ordered my men to keep a particularly strict guard, and forbade them to go into any of the villages. We camped outside, and nothing of note happened, except that the chief was most interested in my gun, and asked me to fire a few shots at a tree to show him how it worked—a request with which I complied.

Starting at daybreak the next morning, the chief himself accompanied me as guide for some distance, and when beyond his jurisdiction I was surprised to find that the people had all deserted the villages along our road. I imagine that what had happened was that the chief had sent messengers on ahead to say that I was coming to fight them and raid their country; or, possibly, the reason was that I had now got to the edge of the Kalyera country, and they thought that I had come to inquire into their behaviour in killing my people and to demand compensation. Although we shouted to them as we went along that we had not come to fight them and waved bundles of grass to show that our intentions were peaceful, none of them would come near us, and we did not interfere with them.

All the country round was thickly populated and under cultivation, like the districts we had already passed through. The chief who had been guiding us had returned to his own village, and we were making very slow progress through an unknown country when two natives came in sight, whom we found had been sent by another chief to guide us to his place. They said it was not very far away, but the native has very little idea of distance, and I thought

we were never going to arrive at his village. I
knew from experience that a native will lead you on
for two or three days with the assurance that you
are close to your destination. Our guides kept telling us that it was just over the next hill, and when
we had got over that it was always just over the
next. I was beginning to get tired, and thought
about camping for the night, when the guides
pointed out a village in the distance, which I could
just make out with my glasses, so we continued our
journey, and arrived close to the village about dusk.
There was a lot of shouting and hallooing, but we
did not go in and camped close together outside.
Practically every man was on guard that night, as
we knew nothing about the people, and could not
be sure that they would be friendly, but though we
heard a lot of shouting during the night nothing
happened, and in the morning the chief came to see
me. As soon as I saw him I liked the look of him.
He seemed a young man, though it is very difficult
to tell the age of natives—they never know it themselves—but I took him to be about thirty. He
seemed to be quite different from any Kikuyu I had
ever seen, his features being more of a European
type, and he had not the thick lips of the ordinary
native, whilst his skin was more of a copper colour
than black. He also seemed a good deal more intelligent than the others I had met, and his people
were not in the least afraid, as most of the others
had been.

The chief's name was Jugana-wa-Makura, and
he had with him a friend, a neighbouring chief,
named Bartier, and we were soon very friendly together. Makura brought his old mother to see me—
a Masai woman, who wore a dress of skins, plentifully hung with iron-wire ornaments. The old lady
was very friendly, shaking hands with me, and telling me that she had heard a lot about the white
man, and that it had been her greatest wish to see

one before she died. They gave me a lot of presents of sheep, and also food for my men, and though I did not allow myself to be taken off my guard by these professions, I found that they were absolutely genuine.

Both of these loyal chiefs, unfortunately, paid for their friendship to the white man with their lives. Some two years after this I came into the country with an expedition sent by the Government to punish the Kalyera for some outrages, and called on Jugana-wa-Makura and Bartier for the assistance of some of their warriors, which was readily given. After our expedition left the country the Kalyera ambushed both these chiefs and murdered them for having assisted the Government expedition. As is usually the custom in such cases, the criminals escaped scot-free, no steps ever being taken by the Government to find out and punish the murderers.

I had had great difficulty in obtaining milk from the previous Kikuyu we had met, as, being very superstitious, they thought that if I drank the milk the cow from which it came would die. I found that this superstitious objection to giving away the milk of their cows prevailed throughout the Kikuyu country. The people themselves use very little, if any, milk for food purposes, preferring to allow the calves to have it, and seldom or never milking the cows themselves, so that butter was unknown in my time among them, though they may now have been taught to go in for dairy-farming to some extent. They were at that time, however, perfectly convinced that to allow a stranger to drink any of their milk was a sure way of bringing disaster on the cow.

Owing to milking not being a general practice, the cows would never give their milk unless the calf was near by, so that if the calf died it was their practice to stuff the skin and place it by the cow when they went to get any milk.

This chief, however, brought me plenty of milk,

and was altogether most friendly disposed, so we camped there for several days, the natives coming in every day to see me, and organizing a big dance for my special benefit. They had heard of my people being killed while going into Naivasha, and told me that the Kalyera were a bad lot and not long before had murdered some Government soldiers who had been sent out to buy food for the people constructing the Uganda Railway.

Being now close to the Kalyera country, I tried to get into touch with some of the chiefs, but they would not come to see me, only sending a lot of insulting messages in reply to my requests for interviews, and saying that if they saw any of my people straying about they would kill them. They did not attack me, however, but I had to abandon my mission to them for the present.

The two friendly chiefs brought me in a lot of food, for which I traded with them, and also several tusks of ivory, which I also acquired. Unfortunately, my own people could not carry all that I had bought down to headquarters, and the chief's people refused to go down with me, saying that they would be killed on the way back, the other tribes being hostile to them; so that the food had to be stored until such time as I could arrange to have it transferred to Karuri's.

My followers having made friends with the people with whom we had been staying, we were all very sorry to leave; but it was imperative that we should return at once, as a rumour had reached me that my people at headquarters were in trouble, and they had sent a message for me to come back as quickly as possible. We had hardly got started on the return journey when it was rumoured among the natives that I had gone on this expedition especially to see the Kalyera people, and that I was returning because I was afraid to meet them. Emboldened by this, the tribe living to the north had attacked my headquarters, killed a lot of the people, and raided the country, burning the villages, and carrying off a lot of cattle, sheep, and goats, as well as some of the women. On hearing this news I hurried back as fast as possible, as I thought it quite likely that they would burn my place. I got back in time to prevent any further fighting, and set myself to calm the fears of my people, who were lamenting the loss of their cattle, and praying me to get back their women. I found that the whole country was up in arms, and set to work to find out what was the cause of all the trouble.

It seemed that my own people had been partly the aggressors, and the old quarrelling had been started again; so I sent out messengers to ask the other chiefs in the neighbourhood to come in to see me. It is the custom always to send two messengers together, as no native will travel alone, and I waited some time, but as neither of the men returned, I supposed that they had both been murdered. So I moved out and pitched my camp at one of my trading stations on the boundary of the country, where I had built a house, which I found had not been interfered with. I hoped, by staying there a few days, to get into communication with the natives, with the object of getting the old men of the district to come in for a shauri. In this I was successful, and we talked over the whole matter of the raid. They said that they had no wish to fight, but the young warriors had got out of hand, carrying things their own way. The result of the palaver was that the women and all the stolen cattle were returned, with the exception of a few sheep and oxen that had been eaten, and knowing that my own people had been the aggressors in the first instance, I did not see that I could take any stronger action in the matter.

However, this peaceful settlement did not please them, and, coupled with my failure with the Kalyera, caused a change of feeling towards me; the people became insolent, and I had to be more than ever on my guard. Things were getting pretty bad, and it so happened that, just at this time, I had to call in a rather powerful headman, who had been causing a good deal of disturbance in the country, to see me; so I sent a messenger to his village to summon him to my camp. He refused to come, and sent back an insolent message, which was heard by all the people round about, and caused a jeering laugh at my expense. This headman was known as a great warrior, who was said to have slept out in the bush at night to kill lions with a spear, and was supposed to have killed several in that way.

I sent further messages to him, but he absolutely refused to come, and began to send threatening replies. He had a following of about one hundred fighting men, and it became a standing joke in the country that he had defied the white man, so that I felt that unless I did something I should lose my influence in the country; I was also getting ashamed to face my own people, who were continually asking if I was not going to bring him in by force. A few days later the matter was brought to a head by a body of about five hundred fighting men turning up at my camp to ask me what I proposed to do in the matter. Seeing that they were thoroughly roused, I said that I would go and bring him in myself. They all wanted to go with me, but I said that I would go alone, and to show that I was not afraid of him, I would not even take a gun, but only a stick or knobkerrie: I took the precaution, however, to have my revolver in my belt out of sight.

I started off with only about ten men, and when we got within a few hundred yards of the mutineer's village, I told the men to stay behind, while I went on to talk to the headman. They had evidently got news of my coming, and were waiting for me, as I could see about fifty men, all fully armed, with the chief in front, drawn up to receive me, and I had no doubt that others were in ambush near by. The man was a fine big fellow, every inch a chief, and I knew that I could only hope to succeed by showing a bold front, bravery being about the only virtue a savage recognizes. As I advanced alone they appeared to be impressed, and a grunt of approbation passed round. The crisis had arrived, and I knew that only sheer bluff could carry me through; so, before the chief could guess my intention, I sprang on him like a flash, and dealt him a blow with the knobkerrie which laid him senseless on the ground, at the same time shouting to his followers to throw down their weapons, as my men had them covered with their guns, and they would all be shot if they attempted to resist. Standing over the chief, with my hand on my revolver, I was ready to face the crowd, but, to my great surprise, they all threw down their weapons. It must be remembered that I was believed to possess mysterious powers, which probably accounts in some measure for their ready submission.

Having made the warriors put all their weapons in a heap, I ordered them to bring in some sheep and goats which they had stolen, and had the chief carried to my camp, while the sheep and goats were driven into my village, the whole of the warriors marching ahead of me till I reached my own people. After giving them a good feed, I gave them a good talking to, and dressed the wound on the chief's head, binding it up with some sticking-plaster; while, to show that there was no ill-feeling, I invited his followers to spend the night in my camp, and return to their own village in the morning.

During the night I heard an awful row, and, rushing out to see what had happened, I found that the two parties of natives had been sitting round the fire, drinking njoi, and having imbibed too freely, had started their quarrels all over again. The old men of the village were fighting with the chief I had brought in, who was defending himself with the flat of his sword. My appearance speedily put an end to the disturbance, and, taking the chief into my own quarters, I ordered my men not to allow any one to go near him. No further trouble occurred during the night, and the following morning, the chief returned with his own people to their village. We parted the best of friends, and for the remainder of my stay in the country he was one of my best men.

Having re-established my influence, I was able to continue my trading, and collected large quantities of food, which I took down from time to time to Naivasha. The possession of cloth and other trade goods seemed gradually to have a civilizing effect on the natives, and they would listen attentively while I told them of our Queen and Government, the big cities of the white people, and the ships which crossed the seas. They were more ready to trade than formerly, and I found no difficulty in obtaining food, which they were only too ready to bring in, in order to procure the cloth and other trade goods with which I purchased it from them.

My chief enemies were the rain-makers and witch doctors, who were jealous of my power, and disliked me because I did not show them proper respect. For anything that went wrong they blamed the white man. When the natives wanted rain, and grumbled because it did not come, these witch doctors said that I was the cause of the drought, and I found that they were gradually stirring up trouble all round me, and trying by every means in their power to get me killed. They knew that they were losing their influence and were not looked up to as they used to be owing to my presence, and they would have done anything to get me out of the country. Of course, they lived by trading on the superstitions of the natives. One of them in particular was believed to have great supernatural powers, and had a reputation for being able to disappear at night, when he was supposed to go to see their god, Ngai. Some support was given to this belief by an incident which was said to have happened one night. A number of the old men were drinking njoi in a hut, when a terrible storm came on. The witch doctor was one of the party. They were all sitting in a circle round the fire, when suddenly there was a tremendous flash of lightning, and the witch doctor, who was supposed to be still sitting among them, dropped through the roof into the middle of the circle. The cunning rascal had evidently crept out of the hut unnoticed by the others, and choosing the moment of the lightning flash, had dropped through into the midst of them; while they, not having seen him leave the circle, were, of course, amazed to see him appear in this fashion through the roof, and quite believed his explanation that he had just come down from their god on the streak of lightning! In spite of the witch doctors, however, the natives were, on the whole, very friendly to me, wishing me to stay in the country.

Things being once more in a fairly settled state, I thought I should like to make a trip north, towards Mount Kenia, to try to make friends with some of the chiefs living in those parts. Wagombi, the powerful chief who lived at the foot of Mount Kenia, had a most murderous reputation, and was reported to be very treacherous Several Arab and Swahili expeditions were reported to have been completely wiped out by him, while the King of Tato, another neighbouring chieftain, a man named Karkerrie, had rendered his name redoubtable by similar murders. I gathered, however, that there was a lot of ivory in that part of the country, and being also anxious to open more food stations, I was not to be scared by the ugly rumours I had heard. Another reason why I wished to make this journey was that I was anxious to see the place where Gibbons's safari had been cut up. So I gathered all the information I could about the district, and talked the matter over with Karuri and his people. They were, without exception, altogether opposed to the undertaking, even the old men seeming to be afraid, and saying that we were bound to be all killed, whilst one of the witch doctors prophesied that I should be killed and never return, and even went through an elaborate ceremony to prove that it would happen. At his request I went into the bush and got three sticks, which I gave to him. Having first waved them round his head, chanting " Lu-lu-lu " all the time, he threw them on the ground, and then, picking up each stick separately, he shook it, first taking hold of one end then of the other. When he had finished this performance he said he could tell me what was going to happen, which, according to him, was that I should have a lot of trouble with the people of the district to which I was going, and therefore had better not go. If I did he assured me that I should certainly be killed and never return.

Of course my people heard what the witch doctor had to say, and in the face of his predictions did not want to go with me. I pointed out that so far nothing had happened to me during the time I had been in the country, nor had any harm befallen any of my personal servants; but my arguments were of no use, they declined to be persuaded, and begged me to give up the idea, saying that they would bring me all the food I could want and that I need not search anywhere else for it. I told them that I wanted ivory, and they hunted up a few tusks which I did not know they had, and these I bought; but I was still resolved to go, so after much persuasion they said that they would go if I would get more rifles, as the people living round Mount Kenia were supposed to have a lot of rifles. They also told me that the trade goods I had were not suitable for that part, where they would prefer brass and iron wire to cloth and beads. I thought, therefore, that my best plan

would be to take down my ivory and the food I had
collected, and when I had disposed of them, to make
a trip down to the coast myself for more trade goods.
I also wished to ask the Government authorities to
let me have some rifles, so I went down to Naivasha
and delivered the food and ivory; then, finding that
the railway was aproaching nearly as far up-country
as Nairobi, which would enable me to take my men
down to the coast without much trouble, after transacting my business I entrained with my savage
followers for Mombasa. They were much impressed
with the evidences of civilization, particularly with
the railway engine, which they thought was alive,
remarking that it seemed in a fever and wanted a
drink. Arriving at Mombasa, they were equally
astonished at the sea and the ships, never having seen
either before.

I was able to buy all the trade goods I required,
and having finished that part of my business, I paid
a visit to the Sub-Commissioner to ask him to allow
me to have some rifles for self-protection. He absolutely refused, repeating what he had said when I
first came to East Africa, that white men were not
wanted in the country. I pointed out to him that
the Arab and Swahili traders possessed rifles, to
which he replied that they had not obtained them with
official sanction! Such was the class of administrator approved by Downing Street for the opening
of a new country!

Before leaving Mombasa, where I stayed only a
short time, I took the Kikuyu on board a ship, which
was a remarkable experience for these people, who
had spent all their lives in the mountains and had
never even seen the sea, let alone a ship, before.
If there was one thing that puzzled my Kikuyu
followers more than another in Mombasa, it was,
perhaps, the fact that everything had to be paid for.
In their own country, when any Swahili traders came
to a village they were accustomed to give them a

sheep for food, and never thought of asking payment, but here, among the Swahili themselves, they found that they could get nothing unless they were prepared to pay for it; above all, they were astonished that any one should have to pay for lodgings, as it was the invariable custom among them to set apart, or more often build, a hut for the use of any stranger whom they welcomed to their villages. They were very soon tired of Mombasa, appearing to be homesick, so we returned to Nairobi, where we camped for a few days, and during my stay bought some cattle, which my people told me would be useful for trading with the natives near Mount Kenia.

CHAPTER VII

Back again in the Kikuyu country—Kalyera raid—
Effect of a mule on the native nerve—Does it eat
men?—Prepare for a new expedition—Dress my men
in khaki, and march under the Union Jack—A
hostile medicine man—Around Mount Kenia—Native
drinks—Treacherous native attack on my camp—
Lucky capture of the hostile chief saves the camp—
Pursuit after stolen cattle—Another attack on my camp
—Change of attitude of natives on account of rain
—Peace again—Bury my ivory—The forest slopes of
Mount Kenia—Wagombi's—A powerful chief—Pre-
cautions—Establish myself and erect a fort

THE return journey was accomplished with considerable difficulty. On arriving at my old
camp at Menzini, where the path branched off to the
Kalyera country, an attack was made on the men
herding the cattle, with the result that several were
killed and some of the cattle driven off. I was lying
down in my tent when the news was brought to me,
so turning out at once, I gave orders for a mule—
which I had bought at Nairobi and given into the
charge of one of my men, with orders to be always
ready to saddle up at a moment's notice—to be
brought, and mounting quickly, I set off in pursuit
of the cattle. The attack had been made while they
were being taken down to drink at the river, and
their tracks were plainly visible, though the cattle
were nowhere in sight. Galloping forward, I caught
sight of them just as they were about to enter the
bamboo forest, with about a hundred Kalyera driv-

ing them on. As I fired my revolver, and came
galloping towards them on the mule—which was a
kind of animal that they had never seen before—they
bolted in a fright. My men had been following me
up in the rear, and we drove the cattle back to the
camp, deeming it unwise to attempt to follow the
Kalyera up through the bamboo forest. After this
we reached headquarters at Karuri's without further
incident.

When Karuri heard that we were coming he sent
men out to meet us, and our return was the signal
for great rejoicings. My mule came in for a special
share of attention, and all sorts of funny questions
were asked about it, such as whether it ate people—
the general impression being that it was some sort
of a lion—indeed, all the natives came in to see it,
and a report was spread about the country that I
went riding about on a big lion. I had brought
Karuri a kettle, and a cup and saucer for making
tea, of which he was very fond, and he was delighted
with them, and, of course, I had also brought
presents for the other chiefs.

During the next week or so I spent the time preparing for my trip north. All the natives were now
anxious to go with me, but I decided to pick only
about one hundred of the best men, and as I had by
this time about thirty rifles, I dressed the men to
whom they were entrusted in khaki suits, which I
had bought on my last visit to Nairobi, and of which
the wearers were very proud. I had also brought a
Union Jack back with me, which I took at the
head of my caravan on all my later expeditions. The
Kikuyu warriors carried their usual weapons, and
the trade goods were divided among one hundred
porters, whom I loaded lightly so that we could move
quickly if the occasion required.

The men looked very smart in their new khaki
uniforms, and with the fifty or so Kikuyu warriors
armed with swords, spears, and shields, and the long

line of porters and camp-followers, it was quite an imposing expedition which set out from Karuri's village one morning. The warriors, armed with native weapons, acted as an advance guard, with myself next, riding the mule; immediately behind were ten soldiers, as my special bodyguard, and following these were the porters, with more soldiers distributed among them. A little farther to the rear were the camp-followers, followed by the cattle, then ten more soldiers, and behind all, a rearguard of fifty Kikuyu warriors.

With orders to keep close together the safari marched out in single file, the Union Jack flying at the head, while Karuri, with the rest of the natives who remained behind, gave us a great send off, though the old witch doctor shook his head as if he still had misgivings as to the success of the enterprise.

The first day we camped at my old food station, where we had defeated the Masai raiders, at the top of the mountain, and resuming the march the next morning, we went through the Chinga country. The natives kept out of the way, though we could see groups of them standing on the hills watching us, and though we shouted to them that we were friends, they only replied with threats, saying that they did not want the white man in their country. All the villages were deserted, and we quite failed to get into touch with the people at all, until we saw some of the old men sitting on a hill-side, to whom I sent one of my men with a present of cloth. He went unarmed and waving a bunch of grass as a sign of peace, and they allowed him to approach them. After he had given each of them a present of cloth, two of the old men accompanied him back to my camp, and when the others saw that they were treated as friends they also came in. I amused them by showing them a looking-glass and several other things that they had never seen before, and explained to them that my object in coming into the country was to buy food. I told them that my idea was to make peace among all the natives, as complaints were coming in to me every day of raids and murders. It was very difficult to understand from their stories whether the things complained of had happened fifty years before or only the previous day, so I advised them to let all those matters drop and start again with a clean slate from now, and I told them that I would do my best to settle any differences that arose in the future. At the same time, I impressed upon them that they must also help me towards this end, and not go raiding and killing each other, telling them that it was only savages that settle their quarrels in that way. To speak of them as not being savages flattered their vanity, and a remarkable thing I frequently noticed was that as soon as a native became friends with me, or with my followers, he immediately called all the rest of the natives savages. It was very laughable in some instances. I have had one of my own men come to tell me that some *washenzi* (savages) wanted to see me, and on going out to see who they were I would perhaps find that the so-called savages were the man's own father and other relatives.

I saw that what I had said about being friendly had impressed them, and in the meantime my followers had got hold of them and were explaining what my policy had done in their own country, so that they could see that I was to be trusted, and consequently made friends with me. After dusk they went home, and it was evident that they had given a good report of me, as the next day the two principal chiefs of the district, Bartier and Henga, came to see me, with about fifty followers. They were both young men and very intelligent for savages, dressed in skins, but wearing no special finery. I gave them a red blanket and a fez each—which was my usual present to chiefs—and they immediately put them on, wearing the blanket over one shoulder like a cloak, the ends being tied on the other shoulder, so that only one side of the body was covered. The effect, however, was rather picturesque, something like the old Roman toga. They were very pleased with their new garb, but it had the result of getting them into trouble at times with the other natives, who looked upon it as a badge of their friendship with the white man.

They stayed in the camp nearly all day, and were very friendly, explaining the features of the country we were going through, and warning me against the people of the district of Tato, and their chief Karkerrie, of whom they gave a very bad account. I asked them if any white men had been there before, and they said no, though they had heard of white men going through the country a very long time ago, but not that part of it.

They had brought me some food and told me that they had some ivory, and they brought me the measurements of several tusks, which they promised to bring in the next day; but although we waited, expecting the ivory, it did not come. They were all still very friendly, however, and so I suggested holding a Pigasangi, but as this was more of a national than a local affair, they said that it could not be done unless they first talked it over with their other people, so I told them that we might be able to arrange for the ceremony on my homeward journey, and also asked them to have the ivory ready so that I could buy it then.

That day we had a visit from the chief rain-maker of the Kikuyu country, a tall, fine-looking man who lived some distance from there, but seemed to having a roving commission and to be able to travel through any part of the country without being molested, all the natives being afraid of him, as they believed that he could bring the rain or stop its coming at will   I very well remember his stalking in, because he was wearing a red blanket and fez which I had given him. On this occasion he arrived, like the villain of the play, just as things were going well, and at one swoop destroyed all my castles in the air by telling the people that it would do them no good to make friends with the white man, as it would stop the rain and bring various other misfortunes upon them. I took no notice, but the natives evidently took him seriously and I had a lot of trouble with him later on.

Striking camp early the next morning, we trekked farther north towards Mount Kenia, where the big chief Wagombi lived. The country continued practically the same, thickly populated and well cultivated, while here and there we could see the sheep and cattle grazing quietly and the people working in their *shambas* (gardens). It was hard to believe that I was in the midst of savages, and that any minute they might be up and cutting one another's throats and my own too; the scene was so peaceful that you could have almost imagined yourself amidst the quiet surroundings of an English landscape.

We had halted to give the men a rest, and I was having some lunch under the shade of a tree—my practice being to start the day with only a cup of coffee in the early morning, making my lunch about midday my first meal—when two or three natives were brought in, who told me that they had been sent by a big chief, who was also a very powerful witch doctor, named Muga-wa-diga,[1] who begged me

---

[1] The name Muga-wa-diga means Muga, the son of Diga, the syllable *wa* being the equivalent of the Russian *vitch* or the Scandinavian *sen*, as shown in Peter Petrovitch or Peter Petersen. In the same way, this syllable is prefixed to the names of tribes, as in Wa-Kikuyu (the sons of the Kikuyu), Wakamba, though in the latter case it has now become an integral part of the name.

to come and camp in his village. Of course I was
only too glad to meet another friendly chief, and
asked them to take me to his village, where we
arrived quite early in the afternoon.

The chief was an old man, very active for his
years, and far more intelligent than the majority of
the natives I had met so far. His appearance marked
him out as a typical witch doctor, and I had never
before seen any chief dressed as he was. His cos-
tume was composed chiefly of the skins of wild cats,
and he wore a hat made of the skin of the colobus
monkey; round his ankles were the usual iron rattles,
while two small boys who were with him carried
calabashes containing various medicines. He had
evidently started off in something of a hurry to
meet me on the road, and came up to me without
any hesitation, shaking hands in a dignified sort of
way, as if the meeting with a white man was an
everyday occurrence. After we had exchanged
greetings, he conducted me to a suitable place to
camp near the village, and also introduced me to his
wives and children, which I thought rather extraordinary for a native meeting a white man for the
first time. I could see that he was very anxious to
make friends with me, and he got his people to assist
mine in building the camp, at the same time telling
us to be very careful when leaving the village to
collect wood or bring in water, as some of the natives
were not to be trusted, and he felt himself responsible that no one should get killed while staying
at his place.

Of course I was always on my guard, and
ordered my men never to go far from the camp without taking some rifles with them, especially as I
found that my friend the chief rain-maker had been
there before me, spreading rumours of what would
happen if they had any dealings with me. But
Muga-wa-diga was evidently not on good terms with
the rain-maker, being jealous of his power, and this

accounted for his being so willing to be friendly towards me.

Finding it a good camp, and being able to obtain plenty of food, I decided to stay there for some days, and in the meantime to try to gather more information about the country and people farther on, while at the same time getting to know more of the people among whom we were camped.

The chief came to my camp nearly every day, and I got a lot of useful information from him. One day he brought his medicines with him, and explained all about them, which gave me a good insight into the art of working magic. Medicine, as we understand it, is not the kind of medicine used by the witch doctor of East Africa, who relies more upon incantations than upon the potency of any drugs to doctor the complaints of those who seek his aid, the ailments he is expected to cure being more of a mental than a physical nature, as, when a native complains that some one has given him poisoned medicine, he really means that some one has put some spell on him to cause something to happen to him. Such is the superstitious nature of the savage that, if one has been told that he is to die at the end of three days, he will actually accept the statement as literally true, and it would have such an effect upon him that, unless the witch doctor could convince him that he had made some medicine powerful enough to counteract the influence of the spell cast over him, he would certainly die at the time stated.

The witch doctor also professed to be able to say what was going to happen to any one who sought the information from him, the mode of procedure in this case being to spread a leopard skin on the ground, and turn out upon it the contents of a calabash containing a lot of stones, lion-claws, arrowheads, &c. These were counted out in sections—somewhat after the style of the game children play with plum-stones in England—and from the balance

remaining after the full number of even sections had
been completed he read the signs. An arrow-head
perhaps foretold that the inquirer would be killed
with an arrow, a lion's claw that he would be killed
by a lion, and so on. They had also medicines for
the treatment of physical ailments, and antidotes
for poisons.

During my visit to Mombasa I had bought a
medicine-chest, which I always carried with me, so
I gave the chief a taste of the different tabloids, &c.
I found that he was very fond of pepper and salt,
and it was surprising to see him take a handful of
pepper and eat it up without winking.

The natives were intensely interested in everything I possessed, and were greatly mystified by the
trick of drawing the heat from the sun, by means of
a lens from my field-glasses focused on their hands,
and it was remarkable how some of the warriors
would stand the pain without making a sign, letting
the flesh burn without appearing to notice it.

When I approached the chief on the question of
a Pigasangi, he promised to talk the matter over
with his people, and suggested that we might also
arrange for the ceremony of blood brotherhood.

Whilst staying here I sent a present to Karkerrie,
the chief of Tato, and also one to Wagombi. We
were a good day's march, in different directions, from
each of these chiefs, and I told my messengers to
say that I was coming into their country on a peaceful mission. Muga-wa-diga said that he would
accompany me to Tato, where, he told me, there was
a lot of ivory; so I decided to go to Tato first, and
then go round to Wagombi's country.

While at Muga-wa-diga's I made the acquaintance
of a young chief named Katuni, or the Lion, who was
by far the tallest Kikuyu I had ever seen—being
considerably over six feet in height—and got quite
friendly with him, and he brought me, among other
things, a lot of honey. All the Kikuyu keep bees, and

you can see the hives hanging on the trees, sometimes five or six on a tree, all over the country. The
hive is made out of a log of wood, hollowed out and
shaped like a barrel, and the ends are headed up just
as a barrel would be. They are about five feet long
by eighteen inches in diameter. The natives ferment the honey to make a drink tasting very much
like sharp cider, which they call njohi, and on which
they manage to get very drunk, as it is highly intoxicating. It is generally made in very large quantities
when the honey is gathered, and the headman of the
village sends out an invitation to all the old men of
the district to come in and have a big drinking bout,
which generally ends in a drunken orgie, when they
all start quarrelling and fighting with each other.
The drink is kept in big calabashes, and the headman
first pours out a hornful, which he spills on the
ground, at the same time saying " Ngai," meaning
" To God "—a ceremony reminding one of the an-
cient libations to the gods. This function over, the
headman first drinks himself, to prove to his guests
that there is no poison in the brew, and then the
general drinking starts. A peculiar and somewhat
unpleasant habit of theirs is to spit on their chests
after drinking, but the reason for the practice no one
could tell me.

I found a similar kind of drink to njohi among
the Abyssinians, who call it *tej*, and the Kikuyu also
have another drink, not quite so intoxicating as the
njohi, and made from sugar-cane instead of honey.

By this time the messengers whom I had sent to
Karkerrie with presents had returned, so we packed
up and moved on towards Tato, Katuni deciding to
accompany me, as well as Muga-wa-diga. The
country continued thickly inhabited, and I noticed
that the people seemed to own more stock than elsewhere. They did not take much notice of us, except on one occasion, when about half a dozen old
men, who had been drinking njohi, greeted us, as we

came round the shoulder of a hill, with a shower of
arrows.

Arriving at last at Karkerrie's village, we were met
there by the chief himself and some of the elders of
the tribe. The country had changed somewhat as
we neared Tato, being less mountainous, and not so
thickly cultivated, but the people owned enormous
herds of cattle, sheep, and goats. They seemed more
like the Masai than the Kikuyu, and undoubtedly
have a good deal of Masai blood in their veins. From
the reports I had heard as to their being such a bad
lot, I was quite prepared for them to try to prevent
my entering their country, but, possibly because they
had heard a lot about me, and also on account of my
having the medicine man Muga-wa-diga and the
chief Katuni with me, they received me in a friendly
way; so, finding a good place near the chief's village,
I pitched my camp.

I had brought about fifteen head of cattle with me,
and, of course, had a lot of trade goods, so I opened
up negotiations with the chief for some ivory. The
value of cattle varies right through Africa, depend-
ing on the number of sheep in the country. Among
the Kikuyu a cow is reckoned to be worth twenty
sheep, whilst among the Caramoja and Sambura
tribes—whom I visited later—it goes up as high as
sixty sheep. I exchanged the cattle at the rate of
twenty sheep for each, and when the natives came in
with the ivory, I would give, say,, the value of twenty
sheep for a tusk measuring two hands. Ten rings
of iron wire, or so many hands of cloth, equalled a
sheep; so that if I bought ivory to the value of
twenty sheep, I would give perhaps five sheep only
and the rest in trade goods.

The iron wire used in these transactions was about
the thickness of an ordinary telegraph wire, while
the rings, ten of which were the value of a sheep,
would be about nine inches in diameter, ten of them
equivalent in value to about a shilling of our money

The standard value of a hand of ivory, in Karkerrie's country, was thus ten sheep, or a hundred rings of iron wire, or sixty hands of cloth. In Wagombi's country the prices were about half these, so that there a tusk weighing from twenty-five to thirty pounds could be bought for about a sovereign and, even allowing for the cost of transport, &c., at an average price of about nine shillings per pound there was a fairly good profit to be made on the deal. In the Wanderobo country, where most of the ivory was in the form of the heavier tusks of the bull elephant —that at Karkerrie's and Wagombi's being mostly from the females—I usually gave a bullock for a tusk weighing from eighty to ninety pounds.

A few details of the native system of measurement may be of interest. The hand, which is their standard of lineal measure, varies with the commodity to which it is applied, but in no case is it the same as our hand of four inches. In selling ivory the hand is the length of the fore-arm from the elbow, with the fist doubled. In measuring ivory a liberal allowance is made for the hollow portion at the root of the tusk,[1] and also for the point, neither of which are reckoned in the length. In buying or selling cloth the hand is practically the same as our yard, being measured from the centre of the chin to the tip of the fingers, with the arm stretched out.

Things were progressing very favourably, and there was any amount of ivory to be had, and I was buying it at the rate of two or three tusks a day, and at eight to ten shillings a pound each tusk would be worth from £10 to £15. I was at first at a loss to account for so much ivory being in the country, as the natives there do not hunt the elephant, but I found that the Wanderobo tribe, who live on the outskirts of the

---

[1] The elephant tusk is more or less hollow for a third of its length at the thick end, measured when extracted from the skull.

country, are great hunters; in fact, they live entirely
by hunting; and the elephants wounded by them, and
getting away, seek cover in the forest, where many
of them die of their wounds, the wounds being made
by poisoned weapons. The Kikuyu, going into the
forest to find wild honey, find the ivory, and as no
trader had been to the country to buy it before, this
accounted for the quantity to be had on my first
visit. These facts may also account for the remarkable stories one comes across sometimes of " elephant
cemeteries. "[1] Certainly, in a long and varied experience of elephant-hunting in various parts of
Africa I have never come across anything but the
slaughter caused by the hand of man which could
account for these so-called cemeteries, nor have
any of the elephant-hunters I have met—and I know
all the chief ones—been able to confirm the
" cemetery " yarn.

One day Karkerrie and his elders came across to
see me, being curious to know all about the white
man and his various possessions. Among other
things in my outfit, I had brought with me a musical
clock, which, instead of striking the hour, played a
tune, and this I had in my tent. After I had been
talking to the chief for some time, the hour came
round and the clock struck up a lively tune. They
could not understand this, and thought there must
be magic about it, so I told them that I could make
it speak whenever I wished, and, unnoticed, moved
the lever. When the hands came round to the hour,
I said, " Now I will make it play a tune." It so

---

[1] A traveller some years since, having come across
large quantities of elephants' skulls and bones
collected together in one place, started the theory that
elephants came to particular spots to die. The
probability is that such places are scenes of the
destruction of a herd by slaughter. (See P. H. G.
Powell-Cotton's " In Unknown Africa," 1904.)

happened that rain had been expected, and as the clock was playing a few drops came. Looking up into the sky, they saw the rain, and at once turned to me and asked if the clock could make rain, so I said, "Certainly, it makes rain all right." They said that it must be a great thing if it could make rain, and seeing that these things seemed to amuse them, I showed them a few sleight-of-hand tricks—never dreaming that they took what I said seriously.

The next day Karkerrie turned up, and said that rain was absolutely necessary, and I must make some for them. I said that the best thing they could do was to bring in plenty of ivory, and go on trading, and the rain would come of itself, as it was not possible for anybody—white or black—to make it rain. They kept bothering me every day, however, to make it rain, and I kept putting them off with the excuse that the rain was coming all right. But, unfortunately, it did not come, and from believing that I could make rain they turned to thinking that I was keeping it away with the clock, and things began to look threatening. The natives would not bring in any more ivory, and I heard rumours that the warriors were coming to attack my camp. In the meantime, unknown to me, there was a plot on foot to murder me, in which, as I found out afterwards, one of my own men was mixed up. It afterwards appeared that he was a native of the very district in which we now were, but had been taken away in some raid to where I had first met with him.

None of the natives came near me, but I knew by the singing, and shouting, and feasting, that something unusual was in the wind, and took the precaution of having every man on guard, and slept myself fully dressed, with my rifle handy, so as to be ready for any emergency. One pitch-dark night about eight or nine o'clock, a day or two after I had noticed the change of attitude on the part of the natives, the crisis came. There had been an ominous

stillness around the camp for some time, when suddenly
the air was rent by a wild uproar, and we heard the
war-cry of the tribe spreading from village to village,
mingled with the shrieking of women and children.
Over all the din the hideous howl of the hyenas could
be distinguished. These animals seem to realize
when there is a feast of human flesh in store for
them, and at the sound of the native war-cry, which
warns them of a fight being at hand, they are always
on the alert. The natives never bury their dead, but
leave them for the hyenas to eat.

All doubts as to the object of this demonstration was
removed by the cries of "Kill the white man!"
which could be heard above the other sounds re-
sounding in the stillness of the night, and it may be
imagined that my feelings were somewhat mixed—
planted there out in the wilds as I was, with a crowd
of yelling savages anxious to cut my throat swarm-
ing round my camp. The darkness added a good
deal to the natural feeling of uneasiness, and I certainly did not feel very sanguine as to the outcome of
this hostile demonstration; but all that I could do
was to see that a strict watch was being kept, and
make the best preparations I could to keep the enemy
out if they should attack the camp. It was quite
useless to think of packing up and clearing out, as
we should have been pretty certain to have lost our
way in the darkness, and have run a greater risk of
being killed in the morning. Further, to have shown
the white feather in this way now would have meant
abandoning my project of going up into the country,
and I was by no means disposed to give up my project. So I set to work as well as I could to build a
kind of fort, using the boxes of trade goods, and
anything else I could get, to make barricades. Having got all my people inside the enclosure, I warned
them not to move out of it on any consideration, telling them not to be afraid, as we should come out of
it all right. All the spare ammunition was placed

ready to hand, and we were prepared for the attack when it should come.

In the meantime, the uproar among the natives had died down and given place to an almost oppressive stillness, only broken now and then by a faint rustling, which told us that the savages were moving about just outside the fort, and, although we could not see them, we instinctively felt that we were being surrounded. The sensation of knowing that the enemy were creeping up all round us was a good deal more trying to the nerves than all the previous noise and shouting had been, and it was difficult to remain inactive as the time dragged on and no move was made against us. I kept the men at work, strengthening the fort, and while they were thus engaged word was brought to me that the chief, Karkerrie, had been seen, fully armed, going to join a body of the natives who were collected some distance away. Acting on the spur of the moment, I called a couple of men, and made my way quietly out of the fort, with the object of intercepting him if possible. I was just in time to waylay him before he moved off, and jumping on him before he was aware of my presence, I made him a prisoner, and carried him back to the fort This was a piece of rare good-fortune, and my spirits rose in consequence. Waiting for the attack, however, was weary, monotonous work, so I went round to each man separately, to give him a word of encouragement, and especially to pass away the time. It was then that I found that one of my men was missing from his post, and it was soon evident that he had deserted. In the morning this man had been on guard over my tent, and I had then noticed that his bearing was careless, and had taken him to task for his lax appearance. I had trained all my men to do things in a soldierly manner, and the leisurely way in which he was moving about had attracted my attention. On my speaking to him, and telling him to walk about properly, and not to go slouching along as he was then doing, he smiled in a way that annoyed me, so I took his rifle away from him, telling him that he would have to carry a load, as he was not fit for a soldier. It was the memory of this incident that made me think of the fellow, and miss him when I was going the round of the sentries, and though I made inquiries, no one seemed to know where he was. I thought, at the moment, that he had deserted on account of my taking his rifle from him, and gave no more thought to the matter.

The night dragged on, without any attack being made, and about four or five o'clock in the morning we could tell, by the different noises heard, and the sound of whispering that frequently reached us, that we were surrounded by Karkerrie's people, who were only waiting for the first peep of dawn to blot us all out. It was evident that the critical moment was at hand, and that it was time for me to act in some way; so I spoke to Karkerrie, telling him that we were surrounded by his people, and that immediately they attacked us, or even fired into the camp, he would be the first man to die. To further convince him that I was thoroughly in earnest, I placed my revolver to his head, and told him that at the first sign of an attack I should fire. The chief had a pretty good regard for his own skin, and, being quite satisfied that I should carry out my threat, he at once shouted to his followers, and told them of the position he was in. Fortunately, his words, to all appearance, had the desired effect, though the Kikuyu were at first considerably surprised to find that their chief was inside the fort, and were, no doubt, badly at a loss to account for his presence there. He had, however, evidently sufficient power over them for his orders to be respected, and they gradually drew off, and things quieted down once again. When daylight came, we could tell by the spoor on the ground, and the way everything had been trodden down, that the

fort must have been surrounded by thousands of
natives during the night.

Karkerrie having assured me that no further attack
should be made, and repeated his professions of
friendship, I set him at liberty, and things resumed
their normal aspect. To see the natives going about
as usual made it difficult to realize that I and my
people had been so nearly wiped out. Nevertheless,
I did not trust the chief, and had spies secretly watching his movements, and ready to warn me of the
slightest sign of treachery. This same Karkerrie,
soon after the country was taken over by the Government, finding that the new Administration were
apparently unable to cope with the raiding of
Wagombi and some of the other chiefs, took advantage of the apparent slackness of the Administration
to attack a safari belonging to some Indian traders,
and looted their goods. But in this instance he had
gone a little too far, and an expedition was sent up to
capture him, and he was deported to Kismayu, a hot,
unhealthy spot on the coast. He did not long survive
the effects of the climate, and the change in position
in life from a powerful autocratic chief to a closely
guarded prisoner. There is now a fort and Government station at his old place at Nyeri, where I had
first come across him.

Although the clock had undoubtedly played a great
part in provoking the natives to attack me, yet it
must be remembered, in the first place, that they were
very much averse to any white man coming into their
country; and, further, being boundary natives—that
is, natives living on the boundary of the country—
they were naturally much more warlike than the
tribes farther in the interior. They were used to
fighting practically every day of their lives, and
accustomed to resent the coming of any strangers into their country. The manner of my coming among
them, so quietly, with the chief Katuni, and Muga-
wa-diga, the witch doctor, had made them, for the

moment, overlook their natural antipathy to a
stranger, and they hardly knew how to attack me.
They probably regretted having allowed me to come
into the country so quietly, and the incident of the
clock gave them the excuse for which they were looking to vent their natural enmity towards the stranger
on me.   This uprising had also happened before I had
been able to get thoroughly acquainted with them,
and consequently I had acquired no influence over
them. I found that they had actually arranged a plot
to kill me, which was to have been started by the man
who had deserted from my camp.   How it was to
have been carried out I never learned, but it is most
probable that he was to shoot me, and the fact of my
having taken his rifle away upset all their plans.
Certainly they had sufficient inducement to wish to
get me out of the way, as many of them, no doubt,
had cast covetous eyes on the quantity of trade goods
and cattle I had with me.   They would not have
hesitated to kill me for such a store of loot, as they
were accustomed to kill Arab traders passing through
the country.   I had not omitted to show them everything I had for trade, as an inducement to them to
bring in the ivory.   They naturally all took a great
fancy to my possessions, but they had not all got
ivory to trade for them, and an attack would have
given a splendid excuse to loot the whole outfit.

I pitched my camp again as usual, and went about
as if nothing had happened, and the natives came to
trade, and mixed with my people as before; but I
was never off my guard, and always carried my
revolver with me wherever I went.

Going on with my trading, I sent two or three
cows out in different directions to be exchanged for
sheep.   It may have been a foolish thing to do, but I
let the cows go out of my camp without sending any
of my own men with them.   I had done the same
thing before, and the sheep had always been brought
in, and it never occurred to me that it might not be

so again; but on this occasion it happened otherwise : the sheep did not come in, and the natives refused to return the cattle. I was rather at a loss how to act, I had such a lot of ivory in the camp. I did not know whether it would be best to leave the camp and go after the cattle, or what to do. Whatever I did, however, must be done quickly, so I decided to leave a few men in camp—about ten askari and fifty Kikuyu—and go after the cattle. The most remarkable thing about the affair was that the cattle had been taken in exchange for sheep in charge of Karkerrie's own men, and his son, and some of the men who went with him, had come back wounded, saying that they had lost the cattle. It was therefore now for me to find out what had really happened, and to recover the cattle.

The wounded men were not fit to go out to show me the place where the fight had taken place, but another of Karkerrie's men offered to come with me and do so, so I saddled up my mule, and started off ahead of the main body of my men to the scene of the fight. On arriving there I found the place absolutely deserted, but, standing on a hill some little distance away, shouting and defying me, was a crowd of natives, who, however, did not attempt to come any nearer. As my own temper by this time was pretty well worked up, I pushed on till I got pretty close to them. They did not shift, so I slackened my pace to allow my own men to come up, and then advance together to within about one hundred paces of them. Seeing, from their attitude and gestures, that they were preparing for a rush down on us, we fired a volley into them; several were killed, and a good many others must have been wounded. This apparently satisfied then, and they did not attempt to put up a fight, but ran away, shouting for their friends to help them to kill us. Realizing that it was useless to try to get the cows back from these people, and feeling rather uneasy about my own camp, I thought

it advisable to return and see what was going on
there; so I hurried back, and on nearing the camp I
heard a lot of shouting and row going on. Being
on my mule, I was able to push on quicker, and got
ahead of the rest to see what was the matter, my
men following as fast as they could. At the same
time, I kept a sharp look-out as I went on either side,
in case there might be an ambush, and at intervals
I fired my revolver into the bushes. On getting in
sight of the camp, I found it was besieged by a crowd
of howling savages, who, I soon discovered, were not
Karkerrie's men, but some natives from another tribe.
Seeing me approach, and hearing my shout to en-
courage my men, they ceased the attack, and
cleared off promptly into the bush. I found that two
or three of my men had been slightly wounded by
arrows, but none had been killed; while the other
side had suffered pretty severely, quite a number of
them having been killed. It appeared that these
natives had heard of my absence, and thought it
would be a good opportunity to attack the camp and
get some loot They had come upon it in a solid
mass, and my men had only just managed to keep
them at bay till we came up; in fact, the camp was
practically surrounded when I got there, and it was
impossible for the defenders to have held out much
longer. Fortunately, I returned in time to prevent the
enemy entering the camp, or all would have been lost.

The unfriendly natives having made themselves
scarce, we settled down into camp again, and once
more things began to go along in the old routine, as
if we had had no unusual happenings.

That day the long-expected rain came, and with it
a remarkable change in the manner of the people
towards me. The day after they came in with lots of
ivory and brought me presents of sheep and goats,
telling me that I was a very great man, as I could
fight and also make rain. They firmly believed that
I was responsible for the coming of the rain, and asked

me to live there altogether, offering to build a house
for me and do anything I wished if I would only stay
among them. Of course, I told them that I could not
stay with them, and soon after brought my visit to
Karkerrie to a close.

Having a lot of ivory, which I did not want to
carry about the country with me, I secretly buried it
at the edge of the forest, my intention being to go on
to Wagombi, the big chief living at the foot of Mount
Kenia. Before I left all the natives were on the best
of terms with me, and said that they were willing to
Pigasangi, while the chief Karkerrie expressed his
willingness to make blood brotherhood with me.
Katuni and Muga-wa-diga had returned to their
villages some time previous to my departure from
Karkerrie's, and I learned afterwards that news of
the happenings at Tato had reached my headquarters
and that we had all been reported as killed.

I had heard a lot of talk about Wagombi, and was
very anxious to visit him and, if possible, make friends
with him, as my aim was to get all that country under
control and put a stop to the fighting and bloodshed,
so that it would be safe for caravans to pass through
it and trade. The natives were beginning to see that
I had their interests at heart and were beginning to
like me. All the way along I had made friends, and
I had hopes that, by means of the Pigasangi and
blood brotherhood, I might get all the chiefs friendly
and at peace with one another. The three ruling
chiefs at that time were Karuri, Karkerrie, and
Wagombi, and I felt that if I could once get these
three to make friends I should soon be able to make
the petty chiefs stop their squabbling. I had already
got a friendly understanding with the two first-
named chiefs, but Wagombi was by far the biggest
and most influential of the three, and if I could get
him to come in the matter was settled and the country
too. My success, so far, was undoubtedly due to my
having Kikuyu natives with me as my followers.

Without them I should probably never have achieved anything at all, but the fact of my having what were practically their own people with me gave the chiefs I met confidence in me.

I parted on the best of terms with Karkerrie, and set out for Wagombi's country. The country we were now passing through was much more sparsely inhabited, and we camped the first night at the headwaters of the Tana River, where, although no natives came to see me, I took the usual precautions for guarding the camp. Very shortly afterwards these precautions were amply justified, and I was made to realize that I was by no means in an entirely friendly country yet. Some of my men, going down without a guard to fetch water, were attacked by natives, and three of them speared to death. They had evidently been ambushed while going through a shamba by some natives who had immediately cleared off, and, though I made inquiries and found traces of a good many feet in the shamba, the murderers themselves were nowhere visible. We buried the three bodies that afternoon, and had no more disturbance during the night. The next morning we had struck camp for the final stage of the march to Wagombi's when we saw a lot of natives doing a war-dance and shouting. Going to inquire what it was all about, I found that they had dug up the bodies of the three men we had buried the previous day, and were having a war-dance over them; so, turning away from such a gruesome spectacle, we resumed our march.

I had, of course, already sent messengers on to Wagombi, to let him know that I was coming, and the news had spread among his own people that I was on the way to pay him a visit. Wagombi himself had come out a considerable distance to meet me, about ten miles from his own village. I found him a fine, tall fellow, in his bearing and appearance every inch a chief, and in his speech a good deal more brisk than any other Kikuyu I had met. He greeted me very heartily, shaking hands in the usual Kikuyu fashion—first spitting in the palm—and had quite a lot to say about himself and the country. He had with him quite a young lad, about ten years old, whom he introduced as his son and successor, and who seemed a very bright little fellow, of whom the chief appeared to be very proud. This lad is at the present time the chief of that district.

Wagombi brought no other followers with him but two or three old men. He himself wore a robe of monkey-skins, and was without any head-dress, while he carried a huge spear. As we proceeded towards the village he told me that he had heard a lot about me, and was very pleased to meet me. He said that he knew he had a very bad reputation for his treatment of people passing through his country, but that he was anxious to make friends with me, and was pleased that I had not brought any Arabs or Swahili with me, as he did not want any people of that sort in his country, and would kill the lot of them. Being some distance ahead of my party, and noticing that we were meeting large numbers of warriors as we went along the road, I sent word back to my people to keep a sharp look-out, and told the chief about my men having been murdered at the last camp. He said that it had been done by his people all right, but that they had been acting absolutely on their own; in fact, he had sent messengers along our road to tell them not to interfere with us in any way, so that what had happened had been entirely against his wishes, and he meant to find out who had done it and punish them.

By the time we had got to his place we had quite a big following, and one old man who joined us by the way must have been the chief's medicine man, as when he first met us he killed a sheep on the road, and at every stream we crossed he sprinkled a little of the dung taken from the sheep's intestines on the river bank and in the stream. (This practice figures

largely in the superstitious rites of the Kikuyu.) He
also sprinkled some on the road as we went along,
at the same time shouting a lot of gibberish. He
had previously cut two rings out of the skin of a
sheep, and given them to the chief and myself to wear
on our right arms, a custom which, it seemed, was a
sign of friendship.

Wagombi's kraal was right at the top of a smaller
mountain which rises at the foot of Mount Kenia,
and from this vantage-ground a splendid view could
be obtained of the country for many miles around.
The morning after our arrival I had an opportunity
of taking in the full beauty of the scene from our
lofty situation. Spread out as far as the eye could
reach was a panoramic view of the Kikuyu country
through which I had travelled, showing the glittering
streams threading their way through deep valleys, the
hills on either side being clothed with trees, and
dotted here and there with villages; while, where the
country was more open, cattle and sheep could be
seen quietly grazing, and the cultivated clearings
could be seen at intervals. Viewed as a whole, the
landscape presented a rugged appearance, with deep
clefts between the mountains, innumerable streams,
and thick forest land; while between the mountains
on the right could be dimly made out the edge of the
Laikipia Plain. We were on the lower slopes of
Kenia, and for a considerable distance up the mountain is clothed with a thick forest, so dense that,
except in a few places, it is quite impenetrable.

The most careless mind must be awed by the
majesty of Mount Kenia, as the eye ranges over its
huge bulk, from the wooded slopes near the foot of
its summit, rising many thousands of feet in the air,
crowned with a circle of perpetual snow, glistening
in the rays of the sun. Surrounded by Nature in her
grandest form, Wagombi might be pardoned for a
conscious pride in his magnificent heritage, which,
owing nothing to the art of the landscape gardener,

yet far surpassed the beauties of any estate to be found in the civilized countries of the world.

I found that Wagombi had a number of rifles, and ammunition for them as well, and all the rifles were in good order. He told me he had got them from the Wakamba, Arabs, Swahili, and that class of people. Describing the Swahili as a foolish lot of people, who attempted to come through his country without taking any precautions, he made no scruple of killing them, and of taking anything they had. One thing I liked about the chief was his absolute straightforwardness about everything. He made no attempt to hide anything, but would tell you quite frankly about all his affairs, contrary to the usual practice of the nigger.

While we were camped there thousands of warriors came to see us, and they came stalking into the camp in such numbers that it was absolutely impossible to try to keep them out, as it could not have been done without using force, and that would have upset everything. Previously in travelling through the country I had always kept men on guard to prevent any one coming into the camp unless first disarmed, but here they came in by hundreds, and I could not keep them out. Knowing Wagombi's reputation, I thought he might be trying the confidence trick on me by appearing so friendly, and took steps accordingly.

I told Wagombi that I should like to build a camp, as it was rather cold, and asked him to get some of his people to help me. He said he would be only too pleased, and the next day his men started bringing in wood and grass; and I then got a lot of them started building a house, and told the chief that it was the white man's custom to put a fence round. As he made no objection, I marked off a big open space round the house, my real intention being to build a kind of small fort; but it was more politic to say that I wanted to build a house, as it roused no suspicion as to my real intention. I had it all planned out in my head, and first of all I had a big circular fence built, just high enough to stand and shoot over. I then told the chief that I had not built this fence high enough, and should have to build another inside it, and as he raised no objection again, I built another, seven or eight feet high inside the first, so that I now had a double fence all round, the entrance to the first being at quite a different point to that of the second. This form of structure would be a great advantage in case of attack, as it would be necessary, after entering the first fence, to walk some distance round before coming to the entrance to the second, and it would give us a chance, in case of a rush, of shooting the intruders before they had a chance of getting into the inner circle of the fort. I also built a tower about thirty feet high, which made an excellent look-out, and had the advantage of enabling the defenders to cover any portion of the fort with their rifles. The plan aroused no suspicion, and they probably thought that it was the way the white men's houses were usually built.

I was rather proud of my tower, and a brief description of it may interest the reader, so I will give it. It was, of course, constructed of wood. Taking four strong poles for the corner-posts, I lashed cross-pieces between them, diagonally, on each side with bark or fibre-rope, which is very strong and lasts for years, and on the top of this framework I built a platform, and above the platform I repeated the process, so that the tower was really a double-storied building, with an arrangement of ladders to reach the upper portion. Wagombi thought that the way I had built the house was quite a good idea, and remarked in a quiet way, " What a good thing it would be to keep a rush of the savages out ! " Curiously enough, by " savages " he meant his own people. I expect he tumbled to my object, as he was a fellow who had all his wits about him, but he made no further comment. My rule had always been never to neglect any precautions, whether the natives were friendly or otherwise; and so far I had pulled through all right. Experience had taught me that to do things in a dilatory or careless fashion was to put temptation in their way, so I never took the risk.

I camped at Wagombi's for a considerable time, and he told me that they had some ivory, and on my expressing a wish to trade the ivory came in plentifully, while the price was quite different to what I had paid in Tato, being very much cheaper—almost given away, in fact, in comparison. In the meanwhile I frequently invited Wagombi to my place, and taught him to drink tea. His headman also came to see me, and we got to be on very friendly terms. After a time the chief mentioned blood brotherhood, and asked me if I was agreeable to join him in the ceremony. I said I thought it would be a very good thing, and then told him about Muga-wa-diga and Karkerrie, and suggested that it would be a grand thing if we could all make blood brotherhood together. I particularly wanted to pull this off, as it would make all the chiefs friendly with one another, and I should then have them under my control.

Later on I managed to arrange the ceremony of Pigasangi, which, as I have explained, is much more of a national affair. Of course, I first suggested this to Wagombi, but did not manage to get his consent without a lot of trouble, and after going very fully into an explanation as to why I was so anxious to bring it about. He had a very strong objection to blood brotherhood with Karkerrie and Muga-wa-diga, and took a lot of talking round; in fact, I only managed the matter eventually by the aid of presents.

CHAPTER VIII

The Wanderobo—Visit from the Wanderobo chief
—Native bartering—A grand meeting of surrounding
tribes for blood brotherhood under my auspices—
Dancing frenzy—Native ideas of a future life—Again
trek for the unknown—Attacked by natives—Chief's
admonition—Decide to visit the Wanderobo chief
Olomondo—Wanderobo gluttony—The honey bird—
Wanderobo methods of hunting—Massacre of a
Goanese safari—My narrow escape—General uprising
of hostile tribes—Rise of the Chinga tribe against me
—My precarious position—Successful sally and total
defeat of the enemy—My blood brother, the Kikuyu
chieftain, comes to my aid with thousands of armed
men—Total extinction of the Chinga people

DURING my stay at Wagombi's another chief
turned up, who proved to be a man named Olomondo, chief of the Wanderobo tribe. The Wanderobo are a race of hunters, who live entirely
by hunting, and inhabit the country round Mount
Kenia and on the great plain adjoining Wagombi's
country, down towards the Guasa Nyero River.
Olomondo came to see me, and, according to the
custom of the country, brought me a present of
honey. It is always customary when making a visit
to a stranger to bring a present, and the recipient is
himself expected to return the compliment by giving
a present of at least an equal value to the one he
has received This man was plainly quite a different
type of native to Wagombi's people, being rather
sharp-featured and practically the same as the Masai

I found out, in the course of conversation, that his clan numbered about six hundred men, besides women and children, and that their kraal was about two days' march to the north-west of us. He mentioned the Maswatch-wanya, and told me that in the course of his hunting he had seen these pigmy people, but had never got into communication with them. It was Wagombi's boast that Mount Kenia belonged to him and the Wanderobo were his people, and joined him if there was a fight. I afterwards found that they were a very timid people, but, judging from the quality of their weapons, I should imagine that they could put up a good fight, Olomondo's bow and arrows being much larger and stronger than those of the Kikuyu, which were like toys in comparison, while as a proof of their ability to use them, I saw Olomondo put an arrow clean through an antelope as big as a sheep. He invited me out to his camp, saying that he had some ivory for sale, and also saying that there was any amount of game out on the plain, and asking me to go hunting with him. This I promised to do later on. Incidentally, he complained of the Kikuyu getting his ivory, as many of the elephants his people wounded strayed away and died in the forest, and the Kikuyu would find their bodies and take the ivory. I told him that I was afraid I could not do anything in the matter, as it was quite impossible to trace the ivory. The Wanderobo knew the commercial value of ivory, and had sold it to the Arab and Swahili traders.

After some discussion it was arranged that Olomondo should make blood brotherhood with me at the same time as the other chiefs, and the difficulty then arose as to where the ceremony should take place. Wagombi, being the biggest chief, naturally wanted it to take place at Mount Kenia, but on messages being sent to Karkerrie and Muga-wa-diga, they refused to come to Wagombi's, saying that they

were enemies of each other, and that they had no
guarantee that they would not be murdered on the
way. I then suggested to Wagombi that he should
send them each a present of a goat or a sheep, but
he said that he would sooner eat them himself. He
was a bigger man than either of the other chiefs, and
it was for them to send him a present first. For some
time there was a deadlock, but I finally got out of
the difficulty by asking Wagombi if he would give me
the presents. He replied, " Certainly, you can have
a hundred if you like. My place is yours, take anything you want." I said that I did not want anything out of the ordinary; if he would give me one
or two sheep, that was all that I wanted; so he had
the sheep brought in. I then said, " All right, you
have given me these sheep, I can do anything I like
with them." He replied, " Yes, they are yours, I
have given them to you." So I then told him that I
intended to send one sheep to Karkerrie and one to
Muga-wa-diga, telling them that they were presents
from him and myself, and I also arranged with them
that we should meet about half-way, and selected a
place for the ceremony. Eventually they all agreed
to this and the day was fixed.

The site I had chosen formed a natural amphi-
theatre, and was a spot I had noted on my way to
Wagombi's from Tato. It was an open space, which
I was told was used at certain times as a market-
place, and I had an opportunity later on of seeing one
of these markets held. On that occasion hundreds of
natives collected there for the purpose of exchanging
their various goods. The noise of haggling and bar-
gaining was terrific. One thing I noticed was that
there was no live-stock in the market, but all other
kinds of produce were to be seen, and it was amusing
to watch a couple of old women arguing as to how
many sweet potatoes ought to be exchanged for so
many beans. One crowd would have loads of calabashes, while another would be selling piles of cook-

ing-pots made of a sort of clay, only to be found in certain parts of the country, which was especially suitable for that purpose; while in another part of the market large quantities of the red ochre—or *siriga*, as it is called—which the natives used for painting their bodies was to be had. Another peculiar thing I noticed was the selling of the native drink njohi, in exchange for a hornful of which I saw a native pay over a hornful of beans. Having no money, everything was bought and sold by means of a system of barter, which was not accomplished without much arguing and haggling, everybody gesticulating and shouting at once.

It was on the site of this market-ground that the ceremony of blood brotherhood was to take place, and it was looked upon as a great event in the country, and the occasion for much feasting and rejoicing. Thousands of the natives attended, each chief bringing a large crowd of followers, while all the tribes in the neighbourhood were fully represented, but no women or children were present. Wagombi took quite a large number of his people, and I took the bulk of mine, leaving only a few in charge of the camp; while Olomondo, the Wanderobo chief, had about ten of his men with him. An immense crowd had already gathered when we arrived, Karkerrie and Muga-wa-diga—each attended by hundreds of warriors —having got there in advance of us. It was a stirring spectacle to see these thousands of warriors gathered together in all their savage glory, their bodies elaborately painted and oiled, and each man armed with spear and shield, while their dress of skins added to their savage appearance. The natives were for the most part standing about, but a few of the older men were sitting down talking matters over, and our arrival was greeted with shouting and singing. Such an event as this was, of course, entirely new to them, nothing like it having ever taken place before in the Kikuyu country, and as it was through my influence that it had been brought about, I was naturally the centre of interest. I had the Union Jack with me as usual, and as we advanced there was a lull in the conversation, and all became quiet and expectant.

Noticing that some had already begun drinking njohi, I advised the chiefs that it would be much better to leave the drinking until their return to their homes, because, as all these natives had previously been hostile to each other, and knowing the native character, I was afraid that they would be getting drunk and starting to quarrel, which would spoil everything. The chiefs readily fell in with my suggestion, and at once put a stop to the drinking. At my suggestion also, all the weapons were placed on the ground, the warriors depositing their swords and spears in heaps, which four of my men were told off to guard.

When all the people were grouped round in a circle, with the chief actors in the middle, I addressed them through an interpreter, and explained the object of the gathering, telling them that they were met together on friendly terms to make blood brotherhood with the chiefs of the country, and that it was for this reason that they had been asked to lay aside their weapons. While this was going on a fire had been lighted, and a sheep was brought in and killed. Each chief supplemented what I had said with some words to the same effect—the old witch doctor, Muga-wa-diga, being the most loquacious, and taking full advantage of the opportunity thus afforded him of indulging his vanity—and then the chief orators of the tribes voiced their opinions in turn. During the speech-making the chiefs and myself were grouped round the fire talking together while the process of cooking certain parts of the sheep was going on. The heart and liver were taken out and cut into little pieces, which were then roasted separately on a skewer, carefully cut and shaved clean before the meat was put on, the result being something like the Oriental mutton kabobs.

When the cooking was finished the orators ceased talking, and all attention was turned on us. Olomondo, the hunter chief, was the first to take a prominent part in the ceremony. Taking one of his sharp arrows, he made an incision in the flesh of each one who was to be joined in blood brotherhood just above the heart. When this had been done the meat was passed round, each one receiving a piece, which he first rubbed in the blood from the wound made by the arrow, and then handed it to his neighbour, who had already done the same with the meat he had received. The meat was then eaten, and this went on until each one had eaten the blood from each and all in turn. This completed the ceremony, and every one turned to dancing and rejoicing, sheep and goats being killed and roasted, and a big feast was held. In the excitement some of my men lost their heads and started firing their rifles in the air, an incident which nearly precipitated a fight, and threatened to undo all the good that had been done. As soon as I heard the firing I rushed up, and at once realized what had happened; but some of the natives thought there was an intention of foul play and began hunting for their spears, and in spite of my explanation things looked ugly, and it was some time before all were reassured and things calmed down.

I advised the chiefs not to delay too long before returning to their homes, as the temper of the people might change, in which case there would probably be trouble. The natives get very excited when dancing, and work themselves into hysterics, when they are not responsible for what they may do. Among my own people I had put a stop to that sort of thing by putting any man who showed signs of getting into that state under restraint at once. Before taking these steps I had seen as many as twenty men at one time all mad with excitement, first one and then another going clean off his head. They would gradually work themselves up into a perfect state of frenzy, until they trembled from head to foot, and after jumping up and down would draw in their breath in great gulps and suddenly grip their spears and run amok. The other natives thought they were possessed of a devil,[1] and their method of treating a man so affected was to bear him to the ground by sheer force, and then half a dozen or more would sit on him. I found, however, that a little salutary punishment very quickly cured them of that sort of thing.

It was pretty late in the afternoon when we left the camp to return to Wagombi's, after seeing that all the others had started for their homes.

---

[1] This devil, whom they called Ngoma, appeared to correspond more to the Christian idea of the devil than is often the case with the deities of savage tribes. The Kikuyu were monotheists, regarding Ngai as a benevolent deity, from whom all benefits came, and to whom they offered sacrifices and paid homage, with a view to favours to come; while Ngoma, on the other hand, was a deity who brought only evil and disaster upon them, and to whom they offered no sacrifices and paid no homage, wherein they would appear to be a good deal more like consistent Christians should be than the majority of the modern professors of that faith, including a good many native clergy, who, in spite of their orders and profession of Christianity, still practise in secret the heathen rites and superstitions of their ancestors.

The Kikuyu are also firm believers in a future life, though possibly from a somewhat materialistic point of view. Their belief is that their "heaven" is situated under the earth, while the abode of Ngoma is above it, and that when they die their spirit goes to the world below, where they will lead a similar life to that which they have left on earth, possessing the same herds of sheep, cattle, and goats as they then had, and being joined again by their wives as they die.

I prolonged my stay at Wagombi's for some time, and continued to trade in ivory, which, as I have said, I bought at a very cheap rate. I happened to have the right sort of trade goods, and the natives were very anxious to deal. I remember that they took a particular liking for one special fancy cloth that I had, and there was quite a run on it. It was a very gaudy material, in a variety of colours, and after they had wrapped a piece loosely round them, they would run about like children, being delighted to see it fluttering in the wind as it streamed behind them like a huge blanket.

I was told that some natives living more down towards the coast had quite a lot of ivory, and that the trade goods which I had still left with me—chiefly iron and brass wire—would be very suitable for trading with them. I also gathered that these people were living in the part of the country where Gibbons's safari had been cut up, and that if I went there I would have to take every precaution, as I should probably find them hostile. Wagombi agreed to provide me with guides and gave me all tne information in his power.

As I was anxious to see the country, and to get into touch with the people with whom Gibbons fared so badly, I arranged to make the journey, and proceeded to get my expedition together. Having buried the ivory I had bought at Wagombi's, as I had done that at Tato, when all was in readiness I said good-bye to the friendly chief, and once again trekked off to parts unknown.

The country was very much the same as that through which I had already passed, being very hilly and thickly wooded, but the natives had heard of my coming and had evidently no desire to meet me. They had deserted all their villages, and I could not get into touch with them at all, although at different times I got glimpses of some of them on the tops of the hills, and though we shouted to them that we

were friends, they would not come near us. As their
attitude was threatening, I came to the conclusion
that they were enemies of Wagombi, and each night
when we camped I took the precaution of erecting a
boma, and would not allow any man outside the
camp unless it was absolutely necessary. The first
trouble came when the men went out to get water.
We were camped on some high ground at a considerable distance from the river, so I sent a good
guard with the party going for water, and as they
were returning up the hill I suddenly heard a lot of
shouting. Taking some more of my men, I rushed
down to see what was happening, and found that the
party was being attacked by a big crowd of savages,
who were shooting at them with arrows. In this
part of the country they use bows and arrows more
than spears, and I actually saw some women armed
with these weapons and using them as well as the
men. Some of the savages had got up in the trees
and were firing on my men as they passed beneath.
and before we managed to clear them out and drive
them away, one of my men had been killed and
another wounded by the arrows. Getting back to the
camp, we found that it was surrounded by another
howling mob of niggers, and we had great difficulty
in fighting our way through and getting in. Once
safely in the camp, we turned and poured a steady
fire into the mass. This fusillade eventually drove them
off, though several very ugly rushes were made before
they finally gave up the attempt to overpower us.

From the height on which the camp was pitched
we could see dozens of villages all round us, and it
was very evident that the country was very thickly
populated; but feeling absolutely safe as long as we
stuck together, we were not alarmed at the hostile
demonstrations on the part of the natives, who still
threatened us from a safe distance, so we slept there
that night, nothing happening to disturb our rest, but
of course a strict guard was kept.

The next morning the natives again gathered round us; but it was a very half-hearted attack that they made this time, however, as they chiefly contented themselves with shouting insulting remarks at us from a distance, only now and then making a combined rush, which we easily beat off. Not that my men did very much damage, as the native has no idea of shooting straight, and it is very difficult to make them understand the sights of a rifle. My men were all right up to a hundred yards, as I had taught them always to aim low, whereas the native is apt to fire high; while the ordinary native who has had no training with a gun is absolutely useless, generally turning his head the other way when he pulls the trigger.

The natives kept up their hostile attitude for some days, occasionally creeping up and dropping arrows into the camp, while we waited, expecting that they would either make friends or put forth a big effort to wipe us out altogether. Our great difficulty was that food was beginning to run short, our supply having been only a small one to start with; so feeling that it was useless to hope to make friends with these people, and that therefore nothing was to be gained by staying there, I decided to trek back to Wagombi's. Breaking camp, we started back, and although the natives shouted at us from a safe distance, as usual, they made no attempt to cut us off, so we got safely back to our old camp. When Wagombi had heard my account of what had happened, he said that, if I liked, he would muster his people and, as he expressively put it, " go and clear up the whole country." I thanked him, but declined his kind offer, as I felt that it was taking on too big a job, and I was also anxious to get back to my old quarters at Karuri's, from which I had now been away about six months. During the time I had been away I had heard no definite news of what was going on there, but it was reported that we were all killed, and that long ago they had given up all hope of seeing us again.

When I declined Wagombi's offer to make war on the tribe that had attacked us, I told him that my idea was to get on friendly terms with the natives without any shooting or anything of that sort, and after I had explained this to him he was rather disappointed with me, and said, " Why all this humbug? The country is yours. What's the use of humbugging about like a woman? " We had a lot of talk about it, and after a time he gave in and seemed to be convinced, remarking that I was a white man and must know better than he what was the best thing to do.

Olomondo, the hunter chief of the Wanderobo, was still staying at Wagombi's, but he and his people were getting restless, and wanted to get back to their families. He was anxious that I should accompany him, promising me plenty of ivory and hunting if I would go with him; so, thinking the opportunity of making friends with his tribe, and at the same time securing more ivory, was too good to be lost, I decided to defer my return to headquarters until after I had paid him my promised visit. I had left some good men in charge at Karuri's, who would be still buying food in my absence, and as I had taken a good supply into the Government stations before I left, I had no fear that they would be running short. I also took into consideration the fact that I was making more money by ivory trading, and this partly influenced me in deciding to accompany Olomondo. In addition to all these reasons I had a strong desire to get more into the wilds and out amongst the game. I was not feeling too well, as the strain of the past few months was beginning to tell on me, and I felt that the change from the thickly-populated district to the practically uninhabited country which was the hunting-ground of the Wanderobo would be very welcome.

We had to take a lot of food with us, and every man had to carry a load, as no flour was to be bought from the Wanderobo, who live entirely upon flesh. I also got a few of Wagombi's people to carry some flour and other things that we should require, but they were to return home when we had decided upon the site for our headquarter camp, as we should make a food station there. Of course, I could have shot plenty of game, but the Kikuyu would not eat it, being in most cases vegetarians.

Having got everything ready for the expedition and said a lot of farewells—Wagombi being very sorry that I was leaving his part of the country—we started off. The first part of our journey led through forest country, and at the end of the first day's march all signs of human habitation had disappeared, and we camped that night at the edge of the forest, while before us stretched a beautiful park-like country, open plain with patches of forest here and there, which struck me as an ideal district for farming. The change from the thickly populated Kikuyu country and the absence of native villages was most refreshing, and I slept very comfortably that night, with the thought of the prospect before us, and awoke to a cool, fresh morning and a beautiful sunrise. Going out of my tent, I revelled in the beauty of the scene spread out before me, and once more experienced the exhilarating feeling of gipsy-like freedom, the liberty to roam where I would at will, hunting the wild game which could be seen in plenty from the door of my tent.

Watering the rich pasture-lands of the plain were numerous cool streams coming down from the mountains, and flowing through the valley to form the Guasa Nyero. All around were the virgin forests, while out on the open plain were many most inviting spots for camping. The whole country was free for us to go wherever we wished, without any fear of interference. One felt that one was in a different world, and wondered how any one who had experienced this sense of freedom from the trammels of civilization could ever wish to go back to the crowded cities, or be cooped up within the four walls of a house. At that moment of exhilaration I certainly did not envy the civilized citizen at home.

After breakfast we set out again on the march, and continued until the heat of the sun began to be oppressive, when we rested for lunch, continuing our journey afterwards through further stretches of most beautiful scenery. Three days' march from Wagombi's we came to the village of the Wanderobo, who had been warned of our coming by messengers sent on ahead of the caravan. They gave us a friendly welcome, but it was evident that they were a very timid people, and I was convinced that, had Olomondo not been with me, I should never have come in contact with them, as they would certainly have kept out of my way entirely. They seemed a bit scared at seeing so many of my followers, but the chief assured them that there was no cause for alarm. Their kraal was a very primitive affair, being simply a lean-to shed, without the slightest attempt at privacy—all the married men and their wives occupying one portion, and the young men and girls another—while I found them the laziest and dirtiest people I had ever met. They will not go out hunting until they are absolutely starving, and when they have killed some big animal, they simply gorge themselves on it, sitting round it, and never leave the spot until every scrap of the meat has been devoured. I was to have an early example of this practice. I had brought with me ten big bullocks, and, as these people had a fair amount of ivory, they were able to buy the whole lot. To my surprise, no sooner had they got the bullocks into their possession than they killed the whole ten at once, and fires having been lighted, a circle of savages gathered round each bullock, and, as it cooked, cut off huge strips of the flesh and ate them, not moving away until each bullock had been absolutely disposed of. A more disgusting spectacle I never witnessed. They live entirely on meat, but have a drink which they make from the wild honey. A remarkable thing in connexion with this honey is that they are often shown where to find it by following a bird, which they call the honey bird. One day, when out hunting, I noticed a small bird of a brownish colour, not much larger than a sparrow, which was twittering on a bush close at hand. Presently it flew towards me, twittering overhead, and afterwards alighted on a tree, still twittering, and the Wanderobo began to talk to it. I had heard of the honey bird before, but this was the first time that I had seen one, and I was very much interested. The natives continued to talk to it, and when it began to fly again, they followed it as it went twittering along, keeping just a little in advance of us, for perhaps a couple of miles, until we came to a hollow tree, where it stopped, and the Wanderobo, saying that we should find some honey there, began chopping the tree away until they found a considerable store of wild honey. After taking the honey out, they gave a certain quantity to the bird—or rather, left some in the tree for it, as they said that if they did not do that, the bird would, on another occasion, lead them on to a dangerous animal or a big snake. Of course this was simply a piece of native superstition, which I satisfactorily proved to have no truth in it, as I took the trouble to test it one day when I had followed the honey bird, by taking every bit of the honey to which it led me, without leaving any for the bird. After flying round two or three times, it went twittering on again for another two or three miles, and when it finally stopped, fluttering round a tree as before, I found that it had simply led me to another store of honey; so I disposed of one native belief.

The Wanderobo women were fairly well dressed—in

skins—but the men wore hardly any clothing at all. When necessity compels them to move they are fairly good hunters, and will creep up to within ten yards of an elephant, to spear it. The spear is fashioned something after the manner of a harpoon, the head being fixed to the shaft in such a way that, on striking the elephant, it becomes detached, and remains in the wound, while the shaft falls to the ground. It would not, of course, be sufficient to kill an elephant but for the fact that it is poisoned; and even then the elephant will often travel a considerable distance before succumbing to the poison. Singularly enough, the poison used appears only to affect the part immediately in the neighbourhood of the wound, and when this has been cut out, the natives eat the remainder of the flesh with perfect safety. Of course, as I mentioned before, the Wanderobo do not get the benefit of all the elephants they wound fatally, as many of the wounded animals manage to wander too far away into the forest to be tracked before they die, and any one finding them gets the benefit of the ivory.

The Wanderobo are very skilful with the bow and arrow, and can easily send an arrow right through a buck at fifty yards' range, while their method of hunting these animals is distinctly novel. Taking a donkey, they fix a pair of horns to its head, and having carefully marked it with charcoal, to make it look as much like an ordinary buck as possible, they then crawl up on the lee side of it until they get close up to the game, which falls to an easy shot. The donkey seems to know the business, and is a very clever decoy.

I learned during my stay that some of the Wanderobo had once mustered up courage to attack some Swahili, whom they had murdered, some of the tribe giving my men the details of their treachery; but, as a rule, they were much too timid to engage in anything of the sort.

One peculiar point about these people was that they all seemed to have a cast in the eye, which I was a good deal puzzled to account for. Whether the meat diet on which they lived so exclusively had anything to do with it, or whether it was owing to their dirty habits—and they certainly were most abominably dirty—I cannot say; but the peculiarity seemed almost universal in the tribe.

I made my camp at a good distance from the village, to escape the unpleasant odour of the decaying meat which was left about, and to escape the vermin, as their huts simply swarmed with fleas, and I well remember the first time that this was brought to my notice. I had been going through the village, and found my clothes covered with what I at first took to be grass seeds; but what was my disgust to find, when I attempted to brush them off with my hand, that I was literally alive with fleas!

Like all the natives, the Wanderobo are very superstitious, and if on one of our hunting trips, we should happen to come across the carcass or skull of an elephant, every one of them would spit on it, at the same time plucking a handful of grass, and placing it on the animal's head, and saying " Ngai " as they did so. This they believed would bring them luck in their hunting. They also were firm believers in the power of human beings to make rain, and in this connexion I had a rather amusing experience. Going down to the river one day for a bathe, I noticed some quartz, which I thought was likely to carry gold; so, selecting some pieces, I was pounding them up and washing them, to see if there really was any gold in it, when, chancing to look up, I saw quite a number of the Wanderobo, hidden in the bush, peering at me in a very curious fashion. I paid little attention to the incident at the time, and after my bathe went back to the camp, as usual. Some few days afterwards we had a shower of rain, and Olomondo and some of the other natives came to thank me for

making it rain. I was, naturally, surprised, and
said : " You need not thank me; I know nothing
about it "; but they said : " Oh, yes, you do; you
can't deceive us, as we saw you making the rain the
other day, in the river." It is just the same if you
do anything which appears to them to be out of the
ordinary—they at once think that you are " making
magic."

I had a splendid time hunting with these people,
and nearly every day, towards evening, I went out to
shoot food for them, the country being like a large
zoo, simply full of every kind of African game you
can think of, including huge herds of zebra, giraffes,
elephants, lions, hartebeest, eland, waterbuck, and
occasional herds of buffalo—enough, in fact, to delight the heart of the most enthusiastic hunter. I
shot several elephants, besides innumerable smaller
game, and two lions—which animals the Wanderobo
do not kill, since, as they cannot eat the meat, they
do not consider them worth the trouble of killing
During our hunting together they killed some elephants, and it was agreed that when an elephant was
killed, they should take one tusk and I the other, and
I eventually used to get both by trading.

One of their methods of catching elephants and
other animals was by the use of pits, which were
dug wedge-shaped, so that when the animal fell in,
it could not turn round or move, and therefore had
no chance of getting out again; while, in some cases,
sharp stakes were placed, point upward, at the
bottom, with the object of impaling any animal that
should fall in. These pits were so cleverly concealed
that one had to be very careful not to fall into them
oneself : the mouth being generally covered with
sticks laid crosswise, with dry grass on the top. They
had quite a lot of these pits, and caught a good deal
of game by means of them.

While out hunting one day, I heard shots fired at
a distance, and thinking it might be some white men,

I sent some natives to find out, and gave them a note to carry to the strangers. They came back saying that they had seen two white men, and given them the note. As there was no answer, my own idea was that my messengers had got close up to the strangers, and then become afraid—possibly at the men themselves, but most likely on account of the note, which they regarded as some kind of fetish. I found out later that the strangers were two Germans, a Dr. Kolb and a Lieutenant, who were out hunting. Dr. Kolb was afterwards killed by a rhinoceros, and his grave, right away on the Guasa Nyero, is marked by huge heaps of stones, I passed it on my trip to Abyssinia, at a later period of my travels.

I stayed some months hunting with the Wanderobo, and so fascinating was the wild, free life, that I could scarcely tear myself away from it; while my followers, who shared the same feeling, had become so friendly with the Wanderobo that some of them had fallen into the habit of eating meat, a thing which they had never done before. This caused a lot of chaff in the camp, and some of their comrades began to call them Wanderobo, which is a term of contempt among the Kikuyu, as the word means a man without anything, a wanderer without any possessions—which fairly describes the tribe in question.

The incident of the note sent to Dr. Kolb was recalled to me some days later, when Olomondo presented himself at my tent, and said that if I would give him some " medicine," he would give me some ivory; as he believed that, if he got the medicine, it would enable him to kill more elephants, while he himself would be safe from being killed. When I asked him what sort of medicine he wanted, he said " the same as I had sent to the white men." I gathered from him that, before I sent the note to them, they had had bad luck, but that afterwards they had killed a lot of game : so I gave the chief a piece of paper, but he was not satisfied until I had

written something on it. Not knowing what to write,
I lapsed into rhyme (?), and Olomondo departed
the proud possessor of a poetical effusion, of which
the following is a sample :—

"I am chief of the Wanderobo hunters.
   Olomondo is my name,
Elephants I kill by the hundreds,
   And thousands of smaller game.
I am up in the morning so early,
   With my bow and arrows so sharp;
Over rivers I glide like a fairy,
   Over mountains I fly like a lark."

There were a number of verses in this strain, but this
specimen will suffice. Olomondo took the paper, and
after wrapping it up carefully, put it in a skin pouch,
which he tied round his neck. I may say that it
must have been very good medicine, for after that
Olomondo had much better luck with his hunting
than before—possibly he had so much faith in its
powers that he went about his hunting with greater
confidence. Later on, it so happened that a Government official got hold of this production, and it
created a lot of amusement. I don't know how it
came about, but doubtless the chief met the official
when out hunting, and asked him for some medicine,
at the same time showing him the paper. As I had
not been heard of for about twelve months at the
Government station, it was reported that I had been
killed; but when they saw this paper, the joke went
round that I was not killed, but was living some-
where around Mount Kenia, writing poetry for the
savages.

At last I absolutely had to get away, as I had
bought all the ivory the natives had, and I was getting
anxious to see how things were going on in the
Kikuyu country; so, after many goodbyes, and promising to come back, I left my blood brother and his
friends and started for Wagombi's country.

Arriving at Wagombi's village without any special incident on the journey, I received a very friendly welcome from the chief, and found that nothing serious had happened in my absence, while the natives all seemed to be on friendly terms. Having picked up the ivory I had buried, I was soon on the march again for Tato, and it was quite a pleasure to see my people and Wagombi's all shaking hands like brothers instead of flying at one another's throats. This friendship was soon to be put to the test, though we had as yet received no warning of the impending trouble.

The same friendly feeling was shown when we arrived at Tato, and it was difficult to believe that only a few months before one tribe was fighting against the other and both were the bitter enemies of my people. I had persuaded Wagombi to send a present of sheep to Karuri, and got the chief Karkerrie, at Tato, to do the same, knowing that the exchange of presents was the surest way to maintain a friendly understanding between the different chiefs. Then, collecting the other ivory we had buried there, we were soon on the march again.

Just after leaving Tato the rumour reached me that three Goanese had been murdered and all their safari wiped out. I gathered that it was a trading safari that had started out from Nairobi, headed by three Goanese, who had with them about forty Kikuyu natives from among some living near Nairobi. They had entered the Kikuyu country, and had been well treated by the natives whom I had got under control, having a really good time until they had entered the Chinga country. It will be remembered that these were the only natives I had never really got into touch with. We had passed through their country just after leaving Karuri's, and for the most part they kept out of my way. As I mentioned previously, some of these people came into my camp, and I had intended to make blood brotherhood—or

rather Pigasangi—with them on my way back. The
Goanese, having had a good time at Karuri's, had,
perhaps, not reckoned on the other natives being
different, and consequently had not taken proper precautions. They were well armed—about fifteen of the
natives carrying rifles, beside themselves—but in spite
of this the Chinga people had for some reason
attacked them and murdered the whole party. This
was the disquieting rumour that reached me soon
after leaving Tato, though I must confess that I did
not put much faith in it, as so many similar rumours
had been spread about myself having been killed, and
I had learned not to trust every report that I heard.
I thought, however, that the Goanese might be in
some difficulty, and perhaps had some of their men
killed; so I hurried up to see if I could give them
any assistance; but the nearer I got to the scene of
the alleged massacre the more convincing were the
statements of the natives as to the truth of the
stories which I had heard.

I did not call at Muga-wa-diga's, as I had done on
my outward journey, but took a shorter route to
Bartier's, and when nearing his village did a very
foolish thing, which might easily have cost me my
life, and, indeed, probably would have done so, but
for the extraordinary instinct of my mule.

Being anxious to meet Bartier to get confirmation
of the statements I had heard from the natives, and as
it was getting late in the afternoon, I left my men
and hurried on ahead. I had never done such a
thing before, but it must be remembered that I was
carrying with me an immense quantity of ivory—
practically every man being fully loaded up with it—
and my anxiety about the Goanese had shaken me
out of my usual caution. Taking with me only one
askari, my gunbearer, an interpreter, and the boy who
looked after my mule, I went on, telling the rest to
follow me as quickly as possible to Bartier's. My
men knew what had happened, and I told them to be

very careful; but still, being in a friendly country, I thought that there could be no harm in pushing on ahead by myself. The path ran between two hedges, which separated it on either side from the cultivated patches of the natives. Suddenly, as I galloped forward, all at once my mule showed a disinclination to proceed along the path, and seemed to want to get off the road into the cultivated patches. This curious behaviour would at any other time have roused my suspicions, but though puzzled to account for the mule's peculiar conduct I did not attach any special reason to it; and, finding that it would not go along the path, I let it have its own way, and turned into the shamba, when it ran along without any further trouble. I galloped along in the gardens for some distance, near the footpath, and had not gone more than a mile when the mule, of its own accord, returned to the road, and I arrived at Bartier's without further incident about five o'clock. The whole village was in a state of excitement, and I quickly received confirmation of the murders, the natives being full of it and appearing terribly afraid that the Chinga people would attack them immediately because I was there. The Chinga people were their neighbours, and the Goanese who had been murdered being, to the native idea, white men, were said to be my brothers. Hitherto many of the natives had believed that it was impossible to kill a white man, and this idea had, to a great extent, kept me free from attack. But now they said that they had killed my brothers, and were only waiting for an opportunity to kill me as well.

Bartier and his people assured me that they were absolutely friendly to me, and that I could rely upon them. It was the Chinga people, with the natives from a part called Mahigga, together with some from a district lying more to the east of us, under the control of my old enemy, the chief rain-maker, who had joined their forces against the Goanese, and I had no doubt that the rain-maker had had as much, and more, to do with the matter than any one else. From what I could make out there must have been some thousands of natives in the business, and they had completely wiped out the traders' safari and taken everything they possessed—trade goods, some cattle they had with them, and everything that was worth looting.

Whilst Bartier was explaining all this to me, two of the four men who had started out with me ahead of the main body of my followers arrived in the village. I had out-distanced them on my mule, and had been feeling some anxiety for their safety. When I saw that there were only two of them, I immediately inquired what had become of the others. It was evident from the state of excitement they were in that something had happened, and they at once told me that their two companions had been killed. Their story confirmed the suspicion which had been growing in my mind that an ambush had been set for me at the place where my mule had refused to keep on the road, and it was no doubt due to the animal's instinct that I had not been killed myself, as my men had kept to the road and so fallen into the ambush. They were going along, they said, when a number of men rushed out on them, and before they knew what was really happening two of their number had been killed. The two men who had escaped could only tell me that they had been attacked by a number of Kikuyu on the war-path, who, rushing out on them, had speared the others and then cleared off, while they had picked up the rifles of the murdered men and come on to Bartier's as fast as they could.

I saw that things were looking pretty bad, and quickly concluded that the men in ambush were some of the party who had taken part in the murder of the Goanese; but whether they were merely a scouting party, spying out my movements, who had got a bit excited and started too early, or whether they had planned to kill me and throw suspicion on Bartier, I could only guess. Bartier assured me that it had not been done by any of his people, and I was quite prepared to believe him, being fully convinced in my own mind that it was the act of some of the Chinga people.

As soon as I had gathered all the details from my two followers I asked Bartier to send out a few of his people to meet my caravan coming along, to tell them of what had happened, and to warn them to be very careful; also, if the two men who had been ambushed were not dead, to bring them in with them, and this he readily agreed to do. My men were not very far behind, and the caravan shortly afterwards arrived, bringing with them one of the men still alive. He had had two or three spears thrust right through his back. He was not yet dead, and I did all I possibly could for him, but he was past human help, and, after confirming the story which the others had already told me, he died in an hour or two.

As soon as the caravan arrived we at once set to work to build a boma, and I realized that I was now in about the tightest corner I had ever been in. With all these men of the Goanese safari murdered, the country was in a state of ferment, and thousands of armed men on the war-path all round us, so that the prospect was not the most cheerful, and I could see that I was in for a rough time, and how I was going to get out of it I could not imagine. As I have already said, I had such an immense amount of ivory that I could only just get along, and it was not likely that I should be disposed to abandon it, after all the months of trouble and worry it had cost me to collect—living entirely among savages, and never seeing a white face for twelve months. At any rate, I meant to make a good fight for it, and determined, if it were at all possible, to win my way out, though I knew that these people, who had already dipped

their hands in the blood of my white brothers—as they
imagined them to be—would do their utmost to blot
me out, if only for the sake of the quantity of loot
which they would get.

The next step to building the boma was to bury
the ivory, and having made this as secure as possible
for the present, I cheered everybody up by telling
them that we should get through all right—that we
had not been travelling in the country for so long to
be afraid now.

It was soon evident that information of our arrival had spread through the hostile tribes, whose war-
cries could be heard on every side, while bands of
warriors could be seen gathering all round us, and
the whole country was soon alive with armed natives,
yelling their war-cries and shouting what they would
do to me when they got me. They looked upon the
Goanese, who wore European dress, as being the
same as myself, and, having had a comparatively
easy victory over them, they confidently expected to
dispose of me without very much trouble, announcing
that they were fully determined to kill me as, they
said, they had killed my brothers. Some of the
natives had dressed themselves in the clothes of the
ill-fated Goanese, and proudly paraded themselves in
front of my camp, while others were firing off the
guns they had taken in the loot. For the time being,
however, they kept at a respectful distance, and we
went on strengthening our defences; but it made my
blood boil when I saw that they had cut off the heads
of the murdered men and stuck them on poles, which
they were carrying about as trophies. I knew what
my fate would be if I were unlucky enough to fall
into their clutches, while my anxiety was increased by
the fact that our stock of ammunition was running
very low, as we had been away from headquarters so
many months and hunting so much that we had used
it nearly all up.

As far as I could learn, the Chinga people could

muster about five thousand fighting men, reckoning in the other tribes who were standing in with them, and the only course open to me was to stand on the defensive. Bartier promised to give me all the help he could, but I could see that his people were terribly afraid, and I could quite understand their feeling, as, if they befriended me, and it should so happen that the Chinga people wiped me out, then they would be in for it. Bartier did, however, give me all the information he could, and assisted me as much as I could reasonably expect from him under the circumstances. At the same time, I could see that he was badly frightened, which, perhaps, was only natural, seeing that the other side were so strong, and seemed quite determined to carry things on to the bitter end. They had already commenced hostilities by murdering my two men, and, fired by their success in wiping out the other safari, were burning to get at me. Since the wholesale murder of the Goanese and their followers they had been rejoicing and feasting and drinking a lot of njohi, and now they were dancing about in paroxysms of mad fury, all alike being possessed with the war fever and ready at any moment to break loose upon us, while we could only wait their first move and take every precaution we could think of

We were camping right on the boundary of the two countries, and could plainly hear them shouting, so I sent out some of Bartier's men, with some of my own, to scout, with orders to hang about in the bush and in the shambas and try to find out what the plans of the enemy were. About midnight news was brought in that a large force of natives was gathered in one of the clearings about a mile from camp, where they usually held their war-dances, and were drinking and feasting and discussing how they should attack us. This threw all the people about us into a state of panic, expecting every minute that the crowd assembling in the clearing would be rushing down on us, though I knew that this would be a most unusual thing for them to do, as savages very rarely rush a camp at night, usually reserving their attack till dawn; still, having had such success before, and having been drinking, I thought that there was a reasonable possibility that they might depart from their usual rule on this occasion. Of course, sleep was out of the question, and everybody had to stand to arms. A large number of Bartier's people were in my camp, and every one was in a state of nervous expectancy. Eventually a dead silence reigned, the effect of which, when surrounded by a host of armed foes, I have endeavoured to describe before. I had experienced the same feeling during the night we were surrounded by the natives at Tato. The feeling of depression was almost unbearable, and was not lessened by the loneliness of my position, out in the midst of a wild country, far removed from any white man, waiting in momentary expectation of the rush of a frenzied horde of yelling savages thirsting for the blood—and loot—of the white man who had so far defied all attempts to blot him out, and seemed only to gain fresh power in the country after every attempt that was made against him. The situation was nerve-trying in the extreme, and after an hour or so of waiting in this horrible silence I wanted to shout in sheer desperation or do anything rather than endure the inactivity any longer. I felt the responsibility for the safety of the followers I had brought into this position and the risk of losing the whole fruits of my twelve months' trying experiences, and could not sit still, but had to keep moving about. Even the movement did not serve to relieve the tension, and I felt that if I did not do something quickly I should be getting hysterical, so I quickly decided to put into action an idea which had been gradually forming in my brain of giving my friends the enemy a surprise, instead of waiting for them to try to give me one.

I at once gave orders for big fires to be made up

and for everything to be done which would give the appearance of the camp being occupied by the whole of my force, and then, leaving only a few men in charge of the camp, I mustered the remainder and stole quietly out, my men being fully armed, to pay a visit to the meeting in the clearing where the enemy were said to be holding their consultation—my object being to teach them such a lesson that they would hesitate to make war on me again. The enemy had evidently never imagined that we should venture to attempt to turn the tables on them in this manner, and in the darkness we managed to creep right up to the edge of the clearing without being discovered, as they had not thought it necessary to put any sentries out. Here we found the warriors still drinking and feasting, sitting round their fires so engrossed in their plans for my downfall that they entirely failed to notice our approach; so, stealthily creeping up till we were close behind them, we prepared to complete our surprise. The moment had come to deal them a crushing blow. Not a sound had betrayed our advance, and they were still quite ignorant of our presence almost in the midst of them. The echoing crack of my rifle, which was to be the signal for the general attack, was immediately drowned in the roar of the other guns as my men poured in a volley which could not fail to be effective at that short range, while accompanying the leaden missiles was a cloud of arrows, poured in by that part of my force which was not armed with rifles. The effect of this unexpected onslaught was electrical, the savages starting up with yells of terror in a state of utter panic. Being taken so completely by surprise, they could not at first realize what had happened, and the place was for a few minutes a pandemonium of howling niggers, who rushed about in the faint light of the camp fires, jostling each other and stumbling over the bodies of those who had fallen at the first volley, but quite unable to see

who had attacked them; while, before they had recovered from the first shock of surprise, my men had
reloaded, and again a shower of bullets and arrows
carried death into the seething, disorganized mass.
This volley completed the rout, and, without waiting
a moment longer, the whole crowd rushed pell-mell
into the bush, not a savage remaining in the clearing that could get away, and the victory was complete. For the time being we were masters of the
situation, only a number of still forms and a few
wounded being left of the thousands who had
filled the clearing a little while before, and we returned jubilant to our camp.

As may be imagined, our success was a great relief
to me, and I reckoned that I had taught them a
lesson which would make them hesitate before interfering with me again : so leaving my buried ivory,
I started off the next morning in an attempt to get
through to my headquarters, feeling sure that Karuri
must, by this time, have heard of my position, and
would send out a force to meet me. Our advance
was made with the utmost caution : halting every
few minutes to search with our eyes the scrub on
either side of the path for any signs of a lurking foe,
and keeping our guns ready to fire at the sight of
an enemy, we went slowly on until we entered the
Chinga country. Skirting the edge of one of the
hills, our way led through a large patch of thick
grass, some seven or eight feet high—an ideal place
for an ambush—and I felt that if we got safely
through this there was little else to fear. Step by
step we proceeded, going dead slow, and making
scarcely a sound; but we had not gone far before
we instinctively felt that our enemies were hidden
in the long grass around us, and our suspicions were
soon confirmed. A black form was seen for a
second, and instantly disappeared. Then shots were
fired, and spears and arrows began to whizz about
our heads, and before we had gone many yards far-

ther, the grass around us became alive with savages. Whenever one showed himself, we fired, and then suddenly, the grass became animated on all sides, swayed and parted, and the horde of yelling black demons was on us. We were fighting at close quarters, and soon every man had his work cut out to defend himself. I was loading and firing from the hip, as fast as I could throw out the empty shells and shove fresh cartridges into the breech. It was a critical moment, and it looked very much as though it was all up with us. So closely were we being pressed that one of the savages had his spear poised over my head, and the muzzle of my rifle was pressed against his body when I fired. My first shot seemed to paralyse him, for while he had plenty of time to plunge his spear into my body he failed to do so, and I had plumped two or three bullets into him before he gave a jump into the air, and toppled over dead. My followers were all equally hard pressed. and on all sides was a writhing mass of black forms, all fighting like devils. We were in a valley, closed in by rugged hills, and chancing to look up, I saw that the top of the mountain above us was black with niggers, who were evidently only waiting to see how those below fared before making a final rush, which must have swamped us; so I immediately shouted to my men to charge up the hill, thinking that if we waited much longer they might suddenly decide to sweep down on us, when our last chance of getting away would be gone. We had by this time stopped the rush of those in the valley, and now, taking the offensive, we fought our way through them up the mountain-side; but when the force on the top saw us coming, they at once turned and bolted, rushing helter-skelter down the other side of the hill. We had had a marvellous escape, and though we had had several casualties, we had come out of the affair with much smaller loss than might have been expected. I saw that it was useless to try to get through

to Karuri's now, as we should have had to fight
every foot of the way, and had practically no chance
of winning through; so we returned to Bartier's.

By this time the news had spread through the
country, and Wagombi and Karkerrie had heard
of my trouble, and had sent some men to help me,
with a promise of more if I needed them. The whole
country was thrown into a state of excitement: the
war fever was at its height: but my blood brothers
had rallied nobly to my help, and big forces of
armed warriors were coming in every hour from the
different friendly chiefs to support me, until I had
a force of several thousands of the finest fighting
men in the country camped at Bartier's.

I was considerably alarmed at the turn events had
taken, especially as the chiefs were determined to
have it out, and threatened to clean up the whole
Chinga country : while the hostile natives had, in the
meantime, collected more followers, having received
reinforcements from some of the other tribes living
to the east; so that I could see that it was absolutely
useless to try to make peace until they had had a
tussle. The people who had come to help me were
also red-hot for war, and scenes of the wildest en-
thusiasm prevailed in the camp of my force. Giving
way to their savage nature, they danced themselves
into the wildest passion, numbers of them going into
hysterical fits, and jabbing their spears into the
tree-trunks in imitation of killing their enemies,
while their breath sobbed out in great gulps. It was
a remarkable outburst of savage, uncontrolled passion, which I was helpless to check.

When the time for action came, this army of
warriors swept through the Chinga country from one
end to the other, destroying the villages, and wiping
out of existence all who opposed them. It was some
time before peace could be restored, and when that
time came the Chinga people, as a force to be
reckoned with in the country, had ceased to exist.

CHAPTER IX

My control over the whole country now complete—Get back with my ivory to Karuri's—Recover all the property of the murdered Goanese—My position recognized by all the chiefs—Violent death of my enemy, the rain-maker—Peaceful rule—Try to improve the agriculture of the country—Imitators of my schemes cause trouble in the country—Troubles of a ruler—Outbreak of smallpox—Famine—My attempts at alleviating the distress misunderstood—Daily routine in a native village—"Sin vomiting"—Native customs—Native hospitality among themselves—Adventures with lions

THE trouble being thus settled, I got my ivory through to headquarters, being met on the road by Karuri, bringing a force to my assistance, my messengers having acquainted him with the state of affairs. From this time on I had complete control of the country; everything that had been stolen from the Goanese was given up, while their murderers had received such punishment as they were not likely to forget in a generation.

When matters had quieted down again, and I had time to review the situation, I took the first opportunity of sending messengers through to the Government, with a full report of the recent occurrences; while I also communicated with the relatives of the murdered Goanese, two brothers who, I heard, were living at Nairobi, sending through to them the whole of the stolen property which I had recovered. I found out later that, through some misunderstand-

ing or other, the heads of the murdered men—which
had been found after the fighting was over—had
likewise been sent in to Nairobi; which, while serving as proof to the officials that the reports I had
been sending in from time to time as to the character
of the natives were not without foundation, was a
most regrettable occurrence, and must, I fear, have
given much pain to the relatives.

The fighting being now over, and the Chinga
people—such as remained of them—having given
assurances of their desire and intention to live at
peace with their neighbours, the country now
settled down into a condition of quietness such as
had never been known before. My mission through
the country had served to produce a spirit of friendship between the different clans and tribes which
effectually put an end to the petty quarrelling and
constant fighting which had hitherto gone on; and
from this time I was looked upon as practically the
king of the country, all matters in dispute being re-
ferred to my judgment, and I was constantly being
called upon to give counsel and advice upon every
conceivable subject which affected the welfare of the
people. The three most powerful chiefs in the
country—Karuri, Karkerrie, and Wagombi—acknowledged me as their leader, and chiefs and people were
now entirely under my control. As proof of the
altered condition of the country, I could now send
messengers to any one of the chiefs or headmen without any fear of their being attacked or molested on
the way.

The reader will remember that I had several times
mentioned an individual who was known as the
chief rain-maker, a man who was by no means well
disposed towards me, on account of the fact that my
influence in the country greatly weakened his position. He went out of his way, on every possible
occasion, to cause me as much trouble and annoyance
as he could; while, in connexion with this Chinga

trouble, I found that my suspicions as to his having had a large share in the matter were perfectly correct. In fact, he had engineered the whole business, both with regard to the murder of the Goanese traders and the subsequent attack on my safari, the former being really a sort of preliminary to the latter, intended to convince the natives that it was quite possible, as well as profitable, to attack and murder a white man, as he carefully explained to the people that the Goanese were white men, and of the same kind as myself. This attempt having failed, like all his other efforts to remove me, he was not content to accept defeat and let the matter rest, but continued to scheme for my removal until his persistence was the ultimate cause of his own death, which occurred in the following manner.

Some time after the Chinga business, reports were brought into my headquarters at Karuri's of serious tribal fighting and raiding in a district some twenty miles to the east of Karuri's, and after a council of the principal men had been held, it was decided that a force should be sent to reduce the offenders to order. Consequently I set out with Karuri, and about a thousand warriors, for the scene of the disturbance. Soon after we had passed the boundary of the disturbed district, which lay partly in the chief rain-maker's territory—for he was a tribal chief, as well as the principal rain-maker—he came out to meet us, with every sign of friendliness, and said that he had brought some of his people to help us to put matters right. Being fully occupied with the matter in hand, and quite ready to welcome any friendly advances from my old enemy, I met him in the same spirit, and told him to let his following of some three hundred warriors fall in with the rest of the expedition, and we continued our march. All went well until we reached the first of the offending villages, where we met with strong opposition, and had to advance our force in extended order to attack the enemy. The order to advance had just been given, and the force were crossing the brow of the hill which stood between them and the enemy, Karuri and myself, together with some of the principal headmen, following them more leisurely up the hill, when I suddenly heard a shot fired immediately behind me, and, turning round, saw the chief rain-maker lying on the ground, while one of the four askaris who formed my personal escort was just re-loading his rifle. On my asking what had happened, I was told by Karuri and the askari that the chief rain-maker had posted an ambush of men with poisoned arrows in the bush near, and was just signalling them to shoot me down from behind, when my escort caught him in the act and fired. Going over to where he lay, I found that nothing could be done for him, as the heavy Snider bullet had gone through his sword—which these people wear rather high up on the right side—and entered his body just above the hip, so that the case was hopeless from the first, as he himself recognized. When I spoke to him he made no complaint about his fate, but begged that five blankets which I had given him at various times might be brought, and that he might be wrapped up in them and buried, instead of being thrown into the bush for the hyenas to eat, as was the usual Kikuyu custom. Having received my assurance that his last wish should be carried out, he died, without saying anything further. Although the man had undoubtedly brought his fate on himself by his treachery, I very much regretted his death, as I thought we were getting on better terms, and he was one of the finest specimens of the intelligent savage—physically as well as mentally—that I have known. Had he been content to run straight and work with me for the good of his people, he would have been able to do a great deal for them.

But we had little time to spare for regrets, for although his death took a great deal of the heart out of his people who had been set to ambush us, they still attempted to carry out his plan to wipe us all out, and as our followers were by this time well over the brow of the hill, we had as much as we could do to hold our own. I managed, however, to get a couple of messengers through the warriors surrounding us, to summon some of our men back to our help. On the arrival of reinforcements, those of the rain-maker's people who were not prepared to give up their weapons and surrender cleared off as rapidly as possible.

Strangely enough, in the course of the same day's operations I was able to do my old friend Karuri a good turn by saving the life of his eldest son, a boy of about eighteen, named Cachukia, who had only recently attained to warrior rank, and was out on his first expedition. We were returning from the reduction of a village where we had met with considerable resistance, and lost rather heavily, when I noticed that Cachukia was not with us, and on inquiring what had become of him, I was told that he had been killed in the final assault on the village. Not wishing to take any chance of the boy having been simply badly wounded and left to bleed to death, I took a few men with me and made my way back to the scene of the fight, where I found the unfortunate youngster still living, but very seriously hurt, having two bad spear wounds in the chest, both of which had penetrated the lung. Although the case seemed pretty hopeless, I could not leave him there to bleed to death, so getting the men to make a stretcher with a blanket and a couple of young saplings, I had him carried back to his father's place where he gradually recovered, and to-day he is as strong and healthy a man as any in the tribe, of which he should be the chief on his father's death.

It may be worth while mentioning that the man who shot the chief rain-maker was so overwhelmed with what he had done, and the possible consequences to himself if he remained anywhere in the neighbourhood of the late lamented's district, or even where his people could easily get at him, that he cleared out of that part of the country altogether, and no one knew where he had gone. I met him some years afterwards on the road in the neighbourhood of Naivasha, when he recalled the incident to my memory, telling me that he had never ventured to go back to his own district.

Soon after my return to headquarters I organized a big safari to take the food and ivory I had collected down to Naivasha, and on this journey I took about a thousand loads of food into the Government station, which they were very pleased to get. I was told that I could take in as much food as I could possibly collect, as some of the flour was required for the other Government stations up-country, where their supply of food had fallen off locally.

During my absence an Indian store had been opened in Naivasha, and having sold my food and ivory, I was able to buy everything that I required for trading at this store, and among the other things I purchased to take back with me were a lot of seeds, including some of the black wattle.

Returning to my home in the mountains, I settled down at Karuri's with a prospect of calmer days before me than I had experienced during the previous twelve months, during which I had been getting the country under control, and now I had time to set about improving the country itself, and got the natives to work making better roads and building bridges across the rivers, and generally increasing the facilities for getting about the country. I also made a very large garden close to my camp, in which I planted the seeds which I had bought at Naivasha, and had the satisfaction of finding that almost every English vegetable would grow well in that climate, while the black wattle I had planted also flourished splendidly, and has, I believe, at the present day grown into quite a little forest.

With the opening up of the country by the railway, new difficulties arose. My own success in the country induced many traders, Somali, Arab, and Swahili, to try their fortunes with the natives, and so long as they stuck to legitimate trading, all went well, but they adopted methods which soon created a strong feeling of discontent throughout the country. In many cases these traders, who had very little in the way of trade goods, represented themselves as working for Karanjai—which was the native name by which I was known—and instead of doing any trading, billeted themselves on the natives, making them keep them, and would often even steal the sheep and other belongings of the Kikuyu. The natives repeatedly complained to me of the misbehaviour of these so-called traders, and when I told them that they were not my people, and that I had nothing to do with them, the natives sometimes retaliated on these men who were thus robbing them. Wandering Swahili, and the other rascals of their kind, came complaining to me. I told them that if they could not get on with the natives the best thing for them to do was to leave the country.

Matters went on in this way for some time, incidents of the kind becoming more and more frequent, until the whole country was in a state of unrest, and as I was continually travelling about the country from one chief to another, I was always hearing of them, and on one of these journeys, I had personal proof of the imposition and robbery that was being practised on the natives by these scoundrels. I happened to be in the neighbourhood of Mount Kenia—where it was still necessary to have a fair number of rifles to go about in safety—and two or three of these Somali traders, who had not guns enough to venture alone, had been following me on the journey, about a day's march behind. It

appeared that at the last village at which they had
stopped they had driven away about sixty sheep from
the native kraal, and had afterwards sat down
quietly to trade these sheep off for ivory in my camp.
As soon as the case was brought to my notice, I at
once ordered them to return the sheep, and told them
that the best thing they could do was to get out
of the country at once, as they could not count on
my assistance if the natives attacked them. It came
to my knowledge that they had made their way down
to Nairobi and there spread reports about my killing
natives and taking their sheep away from them.
The officials were practically ignorant of what was
going on, and I knew that the reports of men being
killed and things of that sort would be believed by
them, in all probability—especially as I was a white
man and the reports were brought by natives. This
meant trouble for me both ways, as unless I got rid
of these men they disturbed the peace of the whole
country; while if I did so they carried misleading
reports to the Government—always ready to believe
anything to the disadvantage of a white trader—and
so, between the natives, the traders, and the Government, my position was no sinecure.

It was about this time that the smallpox broke
out in the country, and for the time·being all my
other troubles were relegated to the background, in
the face of the necessity for adequately dealing with
this awful plague. We were having a shauri, when
I noticed in the crowd an elderly man, a stranger
to that part of the country, and a single glance was
sufficient to show me that he was suffering from
smallpox. I explained to the natives the significance
of my discovery, and told them that if he were
allowed to mix with them they would certainly get
the smallpox and die. They immediately stood away
from him and said that I ought to shoot him, which
to their savage mind was the most natural precaution to prevent the disease spreading. I explained

to them that such a course was impossible, though in view of the subsequent events, the forfeiture of this man's life at that time would have meant the saving of thousands of lives which were lost in the epidemic of which he was the cause. I told the natives what they ought to do to avoid the infection, and arranged for an isolation camp to be built in which the man was placed, telling some of the people who lived near by to leave food for him at a respectful distance, so that he could fetch it for himself until he got better, and also instructed them to see that he did not, on any account, leave the camp. Some days later I was travelling through the country when I again saw the man in the crowd, and in great alarm sent some of my own men back to the isolation camp with him. But it was too late. The disease had already spread to others, and I saw a lot of bad cases among the people, and though I tried to get them all into isolation camps, it was practically no use. When an outbreak occurred in a family they would not report it, but continued to live and sleep together in the same hut, with the result that, in most cases, the whole family took the disease and died. I sent into Naivasha for some lymph and started vaccinating the people. They took the matter in the proper light, and raised no objection, so that I was able to vaccinate thousands of them, which must, undoubtedly, have been the means of saving many lives; but in spite of all I could do, thousands died, many whole villages being wiped out.

One rather remarkable thing about this epidemic was that Karuri's village escaped entirely, not a single case occurring among the inhabitants, which Karuri claimed to be due to certain precautions he took to ward off the evil. He got some sticks and split them down the middle, and then poured some black powder in the opening, afterwards pegging the sticks down across all the footpaths leading to the village. It did not keep people from coming in, and I could not see in what way the sticks could do any good, but Karuri had great faith in their virtues, and as no case of smallpox occurred in the village he took the credit for keeping it away.

Karuri told me that one of the reasons of the respect with which he was regarded by his people was that he possessed a most wonderful poison. If any one even looked at this poison it caused certain death. The secret of this drug, he told me, had been handed down and preserved in his family for two or three generations. The poison itself was kept buried in the bush, one of the tribe being specially told off to guard it and dig up the package when it was required for use; but I could never learn anything about the way in which it was used, and was very much inclined to believe that the whole thing was a legend, of which the old man made use to strengthen his influence among the people. I certainly believe that there was some box or package buried in the bush and carefully guarded, but whether it actually contained poison or anything else I question whether Karuri himself could have told any one. The old man was always very anxious to possess samples of the poisons contained in my medicine-chest, but although I gave him many medicines of various kinds, I always refused to part with any of the poisons, as it is not improbable that he might have taken an opportunity of testing my immunity with some of them.

While on this subject, some account of the native practice of protecting their shambas, or rather the crops growing in them, from thieves may be of interest. Of course this was done by playing on the superstitious fears of the savage, the usual method being to hang some article, such as an old earthenware cooking-pot, an old broken calabash, or best of all, the cast-off earthenware nozzles of smith's bellows, on a bush or tree near the edge of the cultivated patch, and any one pilfering in face of this warning to trespassers was supposed to fall sick, or even die, as the result of his temerity. A similar practice prevails on the West Coast, where a stick with a piece of cloth tied to it, or inserted in a cleft at the top, may often be seen in the cassava patch; and it is supposed that any one violating the protection which this ju-ju is supposed to afford, will, at the least, suffer the loss of some portion of his body, which will rot away and drop off.

The old saying that " it never rains but it pours " was abundantly verified in our case, only in a contrary sense to the literal meaning of the proverb. The failure of the rains in two successive seasons—which was attributed to the white man having brought the railway into the country—brought about a famine which still further depleted the population. The country around Karuri's, being mountainous, was not affected so much as the part to the east of us, on the caravan road, and more towards the coast. At our high elevation, surrounded by the water-sheds of Mount Kenia and the Aberdare Range, we could always rely on a fair amount of rain, though we had had much less than usual during these two seasons. The general famine in the country affected me, inasmuch as the food which I was there to buy found its way out on the borders of the country, and consequently my supplies were cut off. Having occasion to go down to Nairobi about this time, I saw hundreds of poor wretches dead or dying on the road, while some of my men heard gruesome tales of men killing and eating each other in their desperation at the lack of food. No case of this kind came under my personal notice, but I have seen the natives sitting down and boiling the skins which they wore as clothing in the effort to soften them sufficiently to enable them to be eaten.

Numbers of the starving people, when they heard

that food was to be got in the part of the country from which I came, started out to try to get there, but were robbed and killed on the way by the Kalyera people.   It sounds rather paradoxical speaking of starving people being robbed, but the statement is, nevertheless, perfectly correct; as, before starting out, these poor vagrants collected all their household goods and took them along with them, in the hope of exchanging them for food. A few, indeed, had sheep and a few head of cattle with them. Thousands of these people would start off together, and being weak and exhausted with hunger, they fell an easy prey to the Kalyera.

The natives begged me to take them out to Karuri's, and pitying their miserable condition, I agreed to do so, and got together a caravan of several thousands of the starving wretches, among whom were a number of natives who possessed a fair quantity of sheep—perhaps one man would have thirty sheep, and another five or six head of cattle, while, of course, there were numbers of others who had absolutely nothing.   It was pitiable to see these people staggering along, first one and then another dropping out to die on the road.   Before starting out I made it perfectly plain to them that I would only lead them to the " land of promise " on condition that they placed themselves absolutely under my control and obeyed my orders in everything, and this they promised to do.   When I saw them staggering along, almost too weak to drag one foot before the other, and dying at the rate of about fifty per day, I ordered those who had cattle and sheep to deliver them up to me, and each night when we got into camp, I had as many killed as were required to give them just enough food to keep them alive.   Niggers have absolutely no feelings of humanity, and the owners of the sheep and cattle grumbled loudly at my action in feeding the others with their property, which they charged me with stealing.   I felt perfectly justified, however, in the course I was adopting, although I was pretty certain at the time that these people would some day do their best to make trouble for me, by misrepresenting the facts to the Government officials, who, while always ready to accept any statements against myself, were much less inclined to take the responsibility for their own laxity in the performance of their duty. I never ate any of the meat myself, nor did I allow any of my men to do so, so that it could not be said that I had any personal benefit from my action.

As I anticipated, when I took the sheep one or two of the natives deserted from the caravan and went back to the Government station to report that I had been looting their sheep. After much difficulty I got the people through to the Kikuyu country, and distributed them to the different villages, giving them plainly to understand that they must behave themselves.

Not being able at this time to buy any more food, I went about among the natives and started improving my own camp, cultivating the land, making roads, &c. On my visits to different parts of the country I talked with the chiefs and took general note of what was going on, and at the same time bought any ivory that I heard of. Eventually it was brought to my notice that the people I had billeted on the different villages when they were starving, being now healthy and well fed, were bullying and domineering over the natives who had helped them in their time of misfortune. These people I had brought in had previously lived on the edge of the country, in touch with the white man and his civilization, consequently they had different notions and ideas from those amongst whom they had come to live, who had not, as yet, come in contact with any white man except myself. They declined to acknowledge my authority, and endeavoured to assert their power over the natives by taking charge of the villages, and, in some cases, stealing their sheep and interfering with their womenfolk. This led to all kinds of trouble, and the people naturally became anxious to get rid of their unwelcome guests, and they came to me saying that, as I had brought them in, and they were now all right, they ought to leave the country. I explained this to the intruders, but they absolutely refused to go. Amongst the number were some Swahili, who would settle down in a village for a twelvemonth, simply loafing about and living on the natives; and though they called themselves traders, they were really deserters from some caravans. There were also many who were wanted at the coast for different offences, and had somehow or other managed to get mixed up with the famine-stricken people. They knew that I was not a Government official, and as they refused to obey my orders I could not get rid of them. This gave rise to a lot of quarrelling, and a number of people were killed on both sides; so that I could see that the only thing for the peace of the country was to get rid of this bad element at all costs. I therefore gave them three days' notice to quit, informing them that if they were found in the country at the end of that time I would not be responsible for anything that happened to them. They took no notice of my warning, and at the end of the three days the people took matters into their own hands, and drove them out of the country, when, although there was no really serious fighting, some of them got killed and several were wounded. The evicted ones, as I expected that they would, went straight to the officials and complained that I had robbed them of their sheep and driven them out of the country. I was first informed of this by a letter from Mr. Gilkinson, the Government official at Nairobi, and at once sent Karuri and some of the other chiefs into Nairobi to explain the true facts of the case, thinking that a personal interview between the official and the natives would be much more effective than any statement that I, a white man, could make. This idea was apparently correct, as the explanation which they gave proved quite satisfactory—at least, this was the impression which was conveyed to me by the report which they made to me on their return.

The country having been rid of the disturbing element of these alien rogues, I now settled down once more to a peaceful mode of life, going from village to village buying food, and sending in supplies at more regular intervals to Naivasha, where they were very badly needed. There was no further difficulty in finding porters, and a safari of from five hundred to one thousand men went down to the Government station regularly about once every month to take in the food.

Some account of the ordinary routine of my daily life among these people may prove of interest to the general reader. Everybody turned out, as a rule, about 6 a.m., and while I had my morning cup of tea and biscuits, or possibly a dish of porridge made from mawhali or umkanori flour, with fresh milk, the men turned out and cleaned up the camp thoroughly. This over, the men were formed up for a couple of hours' drill and rifle exercise—a training which every man, whether one of the askaris or not, had to go through, so that, in the event of my losing a few askaris, I always had trained men ready to take their places. At first, of course, I had to undertake this daily drill myself, but after a time the native sergeant and corporal became proficient enough to relieve me of everything but superintendence of the parade. Drill was over about ten o'clock, and when I held a court for the trial of any serious cases of crime, or met the chiefs and elders in consultation with regard to measures for the general welfare of the people. By the time this was over it was time for lunch, which was my first real meal of the day, and generally consisted of a dish of mutton—and the native mutton is some of the best in the world. This was sometimes varied by European tinned provisions, of which I always kept a fairly good stock at my headquarters. The afternoon was spent in overseeing the work of the men in my shamba, attending to the repair or rebuilding of any of the huts that were in need of attention, or carrying out improvements in the camp—unless any of the chiefs had come in to see me, in which case the afternoon would be given up to interviewing them. Dinner was served about seven o'clock, in European style, as I had been fortunate enough to get a really good Swahili cook, who could turn out a most appetising meal at very short notice. Of course, I had to dine in solitary state, being the only white man in the country, and about eight or nine o'clock I would turn in for the night. This, of course, was the day's programme at headquarters, though when out on safari I made a point of following the same routine, as far as the circumstances allowed. One day in each week I had a big dance at my place; and this day was practically a holiday, the dance taking precedence of all ordinary work.

The daily life of a chief in times of peace does not present much variety, and the following account of a day out of the life of my friend Karuri is a fair sample. He was not quite such an early riser as myself, usually putting in an appearance to count his cattle and other stock when they were let out to graze, which, owing to the fogs and damp generally prevailing at that elevation in the early morning, was not generally done until about eight o'clock. There was no regular morning meal among these people, who were in the habit of indulging in a sweet potato or a few bananas whenever they felt hungry. Having finished counting his stock, the greater part of the day would be spent in settling disputes and hearing minor cases, which, owing to the native love of argument, were often of interminable length. The old gentleman took no interest in the working of his shambas, which he left entirely to his wives, of whom he had some sixty or more. As the hearing of the cases was accompanied by much drinking of njohi, both judge and litigants were apt to be in a somewhat foggy condition by the time the Court adjourned for the day, which did not generally take place until the time for the evening meal, which, as I have mentioned, is really the only regular meal of the day for Kikuyu. Sometimes the cases were not even closed then, but as soon as darkness came on judge and litigants would adjourn to a hut, and continue the discussion over the sweet potatoes, until it was time for them to turn in, which they usually did about nine o'clock.

One not infrequent interruption to the ordinary routine of Karuri's day was the sacrificial meal of a sheep, in honour of their god, Ngai, which took place sometimes as often as twice or thrice a week. Whether the old chief's fondness for roast mutton had anything to do with the frequency of his offerings I cannot say, but he certainly never seemed to neglect any opportunity which served as an excuse for one of these meals. As I was present on some of the occasions, it may be worth while to give some description of the ceremony, for which no extra preparations were made on my account, as is sometimes the case when white men are to be present at any of their functions.

At the time appointed, Karuri, accompanied by any others who were to take part in the ceremony, went out into one of the " sacred groves " in the bush, taking with them a sheep, which, on arrival at the spot where the sacrifice was to take place, was killed by strangling, its throat being cut directly it was dead, and the blood caught in a calabash, and put on one side. A sort of wooden gridiron was then made, by planting four upright sticks in the ground and laying others across them, under which a fire was lighted, and the sheep, having by this time been cut up, was roasted on this. While the cooking was going on, the blood, which had been put on one side, was put into the stomach, thus making a sort of black-pudding, which was then roasted, and eaten after the meat. The meat was eaten in the Abyssinian fashion, each man taking up the joint, and biting hold of as much as he could get into his mouth, the mouthful then being severed from the joint with his sword, and the joint passed on to his neighbour, who did the same. I managed to introduce one or two slight modifications into the manufacture of the black puddings, by getting them to cut up some of the fat, and mix it with the blood, and boil the ingredients, instead of baking them. No women or children were ever allowed to be present on any occasion when the men were eating meat, as, like the Masai, the Kikuyu do not allow their women to touch meat, and therefore, to keep them out of temptation, never allow them to see the men eat it.

How much religious significance this ceremony had I should not like to say : the fact that it was always held in one of the sacred groves would seem to imply that it had some connexion with their religion, but, as there was no further ceremony than I have described, I always had a lurking suspicion that it was simply an excuse for a good meal of roast mutton, and that the groves were chosen for the meeting-place as being more likely to be secure from interruption from the women and children.

While on the subject of sheep-eating, it may be worth while to mention another of their peculiar superstitious practices, much encouraged by the medicine men, which was known by the somewhat unpleasant name of "vomiting sin." When a man was sick, and went to the witch doctor to be cured of his illness, he was very often told that his illness was due to the anger of God at some sin he had committed, and that, if he wished to recover, the only thing to do was for him to go through an extremely unpleasant ceremony, which I will describe. If he agreed to do so—and I do not think that the man who refused would enjoy much good health afterwards—he brought a sheep to the witch doctor, who, having killed it, wound portions of the entrails round the patient's neck, wrists, and ankles. Then, taking out the dung, he emptied it into a calabash, and mixed it with water, until it was quite liquid. Taking his place opposite the patient, who squatted on the floor with his mouth open, the witch doctor took a couple of small bundles of twigs with the leaves on, and commenced beating the mixture in a bowl with them, and splashing it into the patient's mouth until he was violently sick, when the sin was supposed to be got rid of, and the patient would go away expecting to be quite well in a short time.

On my asking one of these old frauds what became of the sheep, he explained that he would eat it himself, as if any one else ventured to touch the meat, he would die at once. When I said I should have no objection to eating a leg, and was certain that no ill consequence would follow, he replied : " Of course you could eat it quite safely. You are a great witch doctor like myself; but if any of these savages ate it, they would die at once ! "

In the meantime, I made friends, by Pigasangi, with those natives with whom I had tried, on my first journey through the country, to make arrangements for that ceremony, and who said at the time, it will be remembered, they would wait. This enabled me to open up fresh food stations, and altogether my enterprise in that direction was progressing very satisfactorily. The only people who now caused me any trouble were the Kalyera, with whom I had always to be cautious when passing the borders of their country, as they were continually on the war-path, and I heard that they had lately extended their operations into

close proximity to the railway, where they had been
giving a lot of trouble by robbing and killing the
Indians engaged on its construction.

Living, as I did, in close touch with the everyday
life of the natives, I became well acquainted with
their manners and habits of living, and I also
managed to learn a good deal of their genealogy. I
found that the Kikuyu tribe was divided into a
number of clans, or *mahirriga*, each of which bore a
distinctive heraldic sign on their shields. The origin
of these clans was wrapped in mystery, none of the
natives with whom I discussed the question being
able to tell me how they originally came into existence, or what was their real purpose. The word
" clan," as we understand it, suggests unity and
combination, but this certainly was not the interpreta-
tion of the term accepted by the members of the
Kikuyu clans, the members of which were mixed up
indiscriminately, and scattered all over the country.
They all knew to which of the clans they belonged,
and there the connexion seemed to end, so far as I
could gather. The only similar instance of such
" clans " that I can call to mind is the " clan " system which formerly existed among the Red Indians
of North America, where men of different, and often
hostile, tribes might belong to the same " clan," the
clans being known by the names of various animals,
such as bear, wolf, fox, &c.

All the Kikuyu worship a god called Ngai, and I
was given to understand they had also another god,
whom they called Ngoma, though this latter appeared to correspond more to our idea of the devil;
for example, when a native went into a fit of hysterics
at one of their war-dances, as I previously stated
was frequently the case, they said that it was Ngoma
who had entered into him and caused it.

I noticed, in various parts of the country, quite a
number of large trees which had been left standing
alone, and which I took to have been left as land-

marks when the ground had been cleared for cultivation. They were usually to be found on the top of a hill, and stood out prominently in the landscape. I found on inquiry, however, that these trees were looked upon as sacred, and had some religious or superstitious significance. The natives had many other curious beliefs and practices, and had many ways of seeking a favour of their god Ngai. Some of the chiefs, when things did not go right, were in the habit of killing a sheep, which they then took into the bush, and left there as a sacrifice to Ngai; and when a sheep had been sacrificed in this way, none of the natives would go near it, for fear of offending the god. When I remarked that Ngai did not eat, and therefore did not require food, they replied, " Oh, yes, in the morning everything is gone." I took the trouble to find out what became of the sheep, and, as I expected, saw that the hyenas came during the night and ate it; and, to prove this, I shot a hyena one night while in the act of devouring the sacrificial sheep. But when I told them that this was the Ngai for whose benefit they were making these sacrifices, it did not alter their belief. Some of them told me that Ngai lived on the top of Mount Kenia; but others said that his habitation was on a mountain in the Kedong Valley, not far from Lake Naivasha. This mountain, on the summit of which is the crater of an extinct volcano, called Longanot, is known by the name of Kilemongai, which means " the mountain of God "; and it was said by the natives that any one going up this mountain would never come down again, as they were bound to die up there. This piece of superstition probably originated when the mountain was active, and there was every probability that any one going up would have but a poor chance of getting down alive.

When going down to Naivasha I had on various occasions noticed that the natives when they crossed certain streams used to leave a little food at a particular place, generally a few sweet potatoes broken up—sometimes it was left in the bush; and when I asked why they had done that, they gave me to understand that they were performing some religious rite, but I never managed to get any satisfactory explanation of it.

Still more curious, to my mind, were some huge heaps of stones to be seen at certain places as we passed along the caravan track. When we came within sight of one of these heaps a native would pick up a stone, or he had, perhaps, been carrying one for some time in anticipation of coming to the spot, and cast it on the heap, at the same time muttering some prayer to Ngai, as it was on these occasions that he would ask Ngai for anything that he was in need of. It struck me as very remarkable that in my later travels in Abyssinia I should come across the same kind of heaps of stones, while some of my Abyssinian followers went through a similar performance of adding to the heap. When I questioned an Abyssinian as to the meaning of the performance, he would reply by pointing in the direction of a church, which stood on the top of a hill away in the distance, and tell me that, not being able to go to the church to make his devotions, he threw a stone on the heap as a substitute for the performance of his religious duty; and I noticed that while putting the stone on the heap he would bow towards the church. The Abyssinians are, of course, members of a branch of the Coptic Church, and it struck me as possible that the idea had in some way travelled from them to the Kikuyu, who copied it, not knowing precisely what it meant, but understanding that it was some form of worship of Ngai.

I have already mentioned that the practice of spitting plays a large part in many of the Kikuyu customs, and I also found that the same thing prevailed among the people in the district up towards Lake Rudolph, and in fact it was the custom with the majority of the people up towards the north, as I found when I came in contact with them in my later travels. It might seem to Europeans a vulgar thing to enlarge upon, but it was by no means regarded in the same light by the inhabitants of East Africa, amongst whom it is regarded as the highest compliment you could pay a man if you spat on him, or, better still, on his children. On my first introduction to the big savage chief Wagombi, he asked me to spit on his children; and among both the Masai and Kikuyu a friendly introduction was not complete unless spitting had entered into it. They very seldom speak of their children without spitting, and I concluded that the practice denoted respect.

The Kikuyu had a great variety of dances; some were for men only and some for women only, while there were some in which it was the custom for both sexes to take part. There was also one particular dance, which was danced by all the young boys before they were circumcised, in which all who took part were painted white from head to foot, while each wore a kind of toy shield on the left arm and carried, in place of the usual spear of the warriors, a white wand, decorated with white goat's hair. This band of whitewashed young savages went from village to village performing their dance, which they did very well, keeping remarkably good time, and as the postures were gone through each time in exactly the same way and in precisely the same order, it was evident that they had some recognized rule and method in their dancing.

Although the Kikuyu are fearless fighters when their blood is up and will slay their enemies without the slightest compunction, they have a most extraordinary fear of the dead, and would not on any account touch a corpse, for which reason they never bury their dead. I have known a few instances of particularly wealthy or important natives being accorded the honour of burial, but, as a rule, when a native dies, if he happens to be in his hut, the body is left there, and no one ever enters the hut again. If a poor man, or a man of no particular standing, happens to fall sick, and they think he is likely to die, he is carried into the bush at some distance from the village, a fire is lighted, and a pile of wood placed handy so that he can replenish it, and he is then left to die.

The Kikuyu, like nearly all other African tribes, are polygamous, and the general rule seems to be that any ordinary individual may have three or four wives, though, as marriage is simply a question of paying so much for the woman, the number is apt to vary with the man's wealth, some of the bigger chiefs having as many as twenty or thirty. They do not, of course, regard women in the same way that we do, but look upon them more in the light of slaves, the value of a wife being reckoned at about thirty sheep. The women have to do all the work of the family and house, the man himself doing practically nothing. They build the huts, cultivate the shambas, and do all the field work, though at certain times of the year when new ground has to be cleared for cultivation the men condescend to take a share in the work. Each wife has her own separate hut, where she lives with her family, and, if her husband is a big chief, he may have a hut for his own individual use, but, as a rule, he resides with his different wives alternately. They have very large families, and the children begin to take their share of the work at a very early age—the little girl of three years of age relieving her mother of the care of the baby of one year, and, as they grow older, their share in the work increases in proportion. The very young boys have their share in the work too, and may be seen at a very early age tending the herds of cattle, sheep, and goats. This practice, prevalent almost throughout Africa, of making the woman support the family, while the man does little but loaf or fight, is at the root of the often openly expressed

desire of the (so-called) Christian natives that the
Church should allow polygamy among her African
converts—a desire which has been quite strongly
expressed by the " civilized " and educated natives on
the West Coast as among the more primitive tribes
of the East and the interior.

On the whole, the people seemed to lead a very
happy and contented life. They are almost vegetarians in their manner of living, their staple food
being sweet potatoes, although they include a variety
of other articles in their diet, such as yams (which
they call *kigwa*), matama, beans, Indian corn (or
maize), and a smaller grain called *mawhali*, besides
bananas, sugar-cane, &c. They also have a very
small grain like canary-seed, called *umkanori*, which
they grind into flour by means of a hand-mill, composed of two stones—a large one at the bottom, on
which they place the grain, and a smaller one on top,
with which they grind it, after the fashion of the mills
described in the Bible as being in use in the East
thousands of years ago With the flour made from
the umkanori-seed they make a kind of porridge,
which I found very palatable. The natives call it
ujuru, and it combines the properties of both food
and drink, being left to ferment until it somewhat
resembles *tywala*, or Kafir beer, and is very nourish-
ing. When the natives are going on a journey which
takes them any distance from their homes, or out to
work in the fields, they take a calabash of ujuru with
them, a smaller calabash, cut in half, being used as a
cup, into which the liquid is poured for drinking.

The Kikuyu appeared to have no regular hour for
eating, except in the evening, when the day's work
is over. Then everybody, men, women, and children,
could be seen sitting round a huge calabash, cut in
half to form a kind of basin, all helping themselves
from the contents of the vessel, which would, perhaps,
consist of sweet potatoes, or Indian corn, or perhaps
bananas, roasted. In connexion with this custom of

the evening meal, I may here make mention of the open-handed hospitality which is the rule rather than the exception among all the native races of Africa; in fact, I make bold to say that any man who is willing to work at all cannot possibly be stranded in Africa, unless, it may be, in one of the larger towns. I have often noticed a native come into a village at the time of the evening meal, walk up to the circle, and sit down and help himself to sweet potatoes or whatever there might be; and on my remarking to the headman on the number of his grown-up sons I have been told, "Oh, that is not one of my sons; he is a stranger." When I asked where he came from, I was told that they did not know; they had not asked him even his name, and knew nothing whatever about him. He would settle himself by the fire for the night, and go on his way the next morning without his host being any the wiser as to his name or where he came from.

This is only one of the points in which the ignorant heathen so often set an example worthy of imitation by some of the so-called civilized Christians.

They grow a calabash which serves them for almost every household purpose, such as storing liquid, carrying water, or as a drinking vessel. For carrying grain or other purposes of that kind they make a bag from the fibre which they obtain from certain trees, and which varies in size according to the purpose for which it is required; while for cooking or for storing large quantities of water they use earthenware pots, which are made in certain districts of the Kikuyu country in practically the same way as pottery was made in the early days in our own country, being fashioned out of a particular kind of clay and then burnt to harden them. The method of cooking is very much the same throughout Africa, a small fire being made within a triangle, composed of three large stones. An old camp may always be recognized by these three stones, which show where the fire was made for cooking, although all other traces of the camp may have disappeared under a luxuriant growth of grass, several feet high.

The Kikuyu make all their own weapons—spears, swords, and arrows—from the iron which is found in various parts of the country, and which they smelt in the old-fashioned way. I found that the style of bellows used by them was the same as those I had seen in other parts of Africa, being made out of a sheepskin, fashioned to a pointed bag, which, when opened, admitted the air and expelled it again when pressed down. Two sets of bellows were worked together, one with each hand. The native black-smith uses a large stone as an anvil, and possesses a variety of hammers, some of them being simply ordinary pieces of stone, while others are in the form of a dumb-bell, which he grasps in the middle when striking with it. Singularly enough, the tongs which he uses to hold the heated iron are practically the same as those used by the English blacksmith. As the smith is, of course, paid for his labour in kind he charges one sheep for a spear, while a sword may be had for the same price. I found that a lot of the iron-wire which I brought into the country was worked up into swords and spears, possibly because it entailed less labour than the working up of the native iron. In addition to the fighting weapons, they made iron rings and chains, which were worn as ornaments.

Speaking of ornaments, one very characteristic feature of Kikuyu adornment is the enormous size of their ear appendages—they cannot be called earrings. When the children are quite young a hole is made in the lobe of the ear, similar to the fashion in Europe of piercing the lobe for earrings. But they are not content with the comparatively small orna-ments that satisfy the vanity of European women: their ambition is to have the ear ornament as large as they can possibly manage; so the hole in the lobe of the ear is distended by means of a series of wooden pegs, gradually increasing in size until it is large enough to allow of the insertion of a jam-jar or condensed milk tin, which are by no means unusual ornaments for a native to be seen wearing in the ear. And very proud they are as they go about wearing these extraordinary adornments, which one would think must be decidedly uncomfortable for the wearers; they certainly appear so to European eyes, but the natives do not seem to consider them so, and are quite satisfied with the effect.

I do not think that I have mentioned that the Kikuyu cultivate a large amount of tobacco from which to make snuff, for, although they do not smoke, all the men take snuff. Many of the other tribes grow tobacco, but not to such an extent as the Kikuyu, who know better how to cure it than any of their neighbours; in fact, the Kikuyu tobacco has such a reputation in the country that to my surprise I found that the natives about Lake Rudolph, and even right round as far as Abyssinia, were inquiring for Kikuyu tobacco.

The most striking incidents of my life at this time while I was living among the Kikuyu were occurrences which took place on some of the journeys down to Naivasha with the caravans taking in food. On two occasions while marching down I had people killed by elephants, which were fairly numerous in the bamboo forest at certain times of the year. With a safari of a thousand men the long line of porters extended for about five or six miles, winding through the forest like a huge serpent and tailing away into the distance; and occasionally, when an elephant crossed the path, one of the stragglers in the rear would find himself suddenly encircled round the body by an elephant's trunk and hurled several feet in the air, to be trampled to death under the ponderous brute's feet when his body crashed to the ground again. The porters nearest to him would then set up a shout, which was repeated all along the line until it reached me, when I would immediately rush back as quickly as possible, only to find, when I at length reached the spot, that the elephant had been lost in the forest long before I got there, the bamboos growing so thickly that it could not be seen for any great distance. Incidents of this sort happened on two occasions on the road to Naivasha.

The forest was full of animal life, including a fair number of bushbuck and some specimens of a very rare kind of buck known as the bongo. The bongo has horns like those of the bushbuck, but very much larger, curving backwards with one or two spiral twists, and ending in a point tipped with white. The hide is reddish in colour, with very narrow white stripes. There are a few of the species to be found at the Ravine. Among the other inhabitants of the forest I have seen wart hogs and wild pigs, while the colobus monkey makes his home in the bamboo forest, and is regarded as sacred by the natives, who, as far as I could understand, were in the habit of placing sacrifices in the forest, which these monkeys came and ate. The skin of the colobus monkey is greatly prized, the hair being very long, while the upper part of the body is jet black, with a white stripe down each side, widening towards the tail, which is also white, the result of the peculiar arrangement of the two colours being to give the animal a very curious appearance. Guinea-fowl were very plentiful, and I also saw some partridges, but was never tempted to shoot any. At times we had great difficulty in getting through the forest, in consequence of the elephants having pulled down a number of the bamboos and thus blocked the path, and we frequently had to make a new path before we could proeed on our journey.

I had some personal experiences with animals in the forest, which added a little excitement to the journeys. On one occasion as we were going along some of the boys pointed into the bush, saying,

" Yama," which is the Swahili word for meat, and is
applied indiscriminately to any animal. It was
getting dusk, and, peering into the bush, I could see
something dark moving, but not being able in the
half darkness to see what it was, I thought that
the best thing to do was to try the effect of a
bullet on it. I had no sooner fired than the
animal charged out on me, and I saw that it was
a huge rhinoceros. Having only soft-nosed bullets,
my shot had not injured it, and as it was only
about ten paces from where I was standing I
had only just time to spring out of the way before
it blundered past me. Immediately every man
dropped his load and sprang up the nearest tree, while
the rhino, after passing me, slowed down and began
sniffing about among the loads which the porters had
thrown to the ground in their hurry to get to places
of safety. Although I knew that unless I could hit
him in a vulnerable spot it was no use firing, I gave
him a few shots at random, which had the effect of
driving him off.

One night we had a peculiar experience with a lion.
With such a number of porters it was impossible to
provide tents for all the men, so we used to bivouac at
nights either on the edge of the forest or in some deep
ravine where we were sheltered from the wind. On
the particular evening of which I am writing we were
settled for the night in a ravine, and I was suddenly
aroused from my sleep by shouting, howling, and the
waving of firebrands, while at the same moment a
huge boulder came crashing through my tent.
Thinking that it was at least an attack by the Kalyera
or Masai or some of the other natives, I rushed out of
my tent to find that what had really happened
was that a lion had come prowling round the
camp, and was in the act of springing on some
man sleeping below when he dislodged a boulder from
the overhanging ledge on which he was crouching for
the spring, which had dropped on my tent. The noise

made by the porters and the stone slipping from under its feet must have scared the animal, as he made off just as I came out. There were quite a number of lions on the Kinangop Plain and near Naivasha, so we always made big fires at night to guard the camp, and never had the bad luck to have any one taken. One day a Masai reported that a lion had been into the kraal and had killed thirty sheep, every one of which had been killed by a tap of his paw, but none of them had been eaten.

I was told of a remarkable occurrence which had taken place at Naivasha. One of the officials there had a white horse, and one night a prowling lion sprang on its back. Hearing the noise, one of the soldiers fired, and, although it was too dark to take an accurate aim, he was fortunate enough to hit the lion, which dropped off the horse's back dead, while the horse was none the worse, save for a few scratches from the lion's claws. Of course, it was purely a chance shot, as it was much too dark for the man to see clearly, and that was probably how he came to kill the lion—niggers being, as a rule, atrocious shots with a rifle.

When going into Naivasha, the country around there being considered practically safe, I often used to gallop on ahead of the caravan on my mule, taking only a couple of boys with me, to let them know that the safari was coming and to make arrangements for it on arrival. On one of these occasions, when crossing the Kinangop Plain, I had a rather lively experience with a leopard. After being cooped up in the hills for so long it was a pleasure to get a good gallop over the open plain, and I was riding along, thoroughly enjoying the exercise, when, chancing to look round to see how far my gunbearer was behind, I saw a leopard following me at a distance of about thirty yards. I at once pulled up, when the leopard immediately followed my example, and, after looking at one another for a minute or two, the animal began walking slowly up and down, swishing its tail about, and looking for all the world like a big cat, but it did not offer to approach any nearer. This went on for some time, until I at last saw the boy come into sight, carrying my gun; but directly he saw the leopard, which was between us, he was afraid to come any farther, and though I waved my hand to him to make his way round to me, he would not move. The leopard still continued to march up and down, until presently it saw the boy and appeared to hesitate, as if wondering which of us to attack, though my mule had evidently been the first attraction. The animal seemed to be puzzled at seeing me on its back, and apparently did not quite know what to make of it. Seeing that the boy was too scared to come to me, I made a detour—the leopard still following me at about the same distance—and as soon as I reached the boy I dismounted quickly, and, taking my gun from him, fired at the animal, and evidently hit him, for he gave a bound and cleared off. Whilst he was making off as fast as he could go I managed to get two more shots in, and followed him until he disappeared into some bushes. Knowing that one does not stand a chance with a wounded leopard in a bush, I hesitated to follow, but I did not like to leave it; so I tried, by throwing stones and in other ways, to find out whether it was still alive and likely to be dangerous or whether I had actually finished it. Hearing no movement, I plucked up courage, after some manœuvring, to go into the bush. Moving as stealthily as I could, not knowing whether the animal might not spring out on me at any moment, I worked my way cautiously in, but I had not gone many yards before I found it lying stone dead.

A wounded leopard is one of the most dangerous animals in the world to tackle, and two of my friends were lamed for life as a result of following up leopards which they had only wounded. One was a man named Hall, and the other a hunter named Vincent. The latter had wounded a leopard, and was following it into the bush when the animal sprang at him suddenly and tried to seize him by the throat, and a hand-to-hand fight ensued. Vincent managed to throw the animal off and fired at it, but it flew at him again, and the struggle went on until he had emptied his magazine into the brute's body, having fired ten rounds into it. The leopard had managed in the struggle to fasten its teeth in his knee and to bite him very severely. As the result blood poisoning set in, and Vincent was laid up for several months and was lamed for life.

CHAPTER X

Government send an expedition into my country to take over the administration—Go with my followers to meet the Government officials—Am asked to disarm my followers by the Government officials—Consent to this, and am then put under arrest—Am charged with "dacoity"—Am sent down to Mombasa to be tried, and placed in the jail—Am released on bail—Tried and acquitted—I am appointed intelligence officer, and guide to a Government expedition into the Kikuyu country

I HAD been living and trading in the Kikuyu country for something like two and a half years now, and during the whole of that time had had no white visitors in the country, when one day the news was brought in that some white men had come into my neighbourhood. News of an event of this sort of course spreads very quickly, and the natives reported to me that at Mberri, about thirty miles to the east of my headquarters, two white men were camping with a lot of troops, and had commenced to build a fort. When I had made a few inquiries, I found that they were Government officials, who had come out to take over the country, and when I was satisfied of this, as soon as I could spare the time, I called all the chiefs together and told them that these two white men were evidently officers of the Government and had come to take the country over, and that as it had hitherto fallen to my lot to settle quarrels and disputes and generally manage the affairs of the whole country, so now, I explained, these new-comers had been sent for that purpose and to take my place. I gave the chiefs some days' notice to be ready to go up with me, and said that I would take them up and introduce them to the officials.

When the time came to start for Mberri all the chiefs did not turn up, but I found that a good number of the thirty-six who at that time looked to me as their head were ready to accompany me. Each chief brought some of his followers with him, and we started off with about one thousand men, and, as it was too far for a day's march, I camped after travelling about three-parts of the way to the fort. Resuming our journey the next morning, we had nearly covered the remaining portion of the distance, when it suddenly struck me that if such a large body of armed natives were seen approaching the fort without any notice of their coming having been received, they might easily be mistaken for a hostile force coming to attack the new station, so I called a halt about two or three miles from the fort, and, leaving the natives behind, went on ahead to report their arrival.

On reaching Mberri I met one of the officers in charge of the fort, who turned out to be a man I knew very well, having met him previously at Fort Smith, when he was in charge of that station; while the other was also known to me through my having been in communication with him on several occasions respecting certain happenings in the Kikuyu country. The two officials received me in a friendly way and invited me to have some breakfast with them. Having reported to them that I had brought in a number of friendly chiefs to introduce to them, and explained my mission, I sent a man back to my people to tell them to come on in, and was still at breakfast when I heard a lot of shouting and talking, and went out to see what was the matter. On asking what the fuss was about, I was told that my askaris were being placed under arrest, and when I inquired what they had been doing, was told that they had no right to be in uniform. As a matter of fact they were not wearing a Government uniform, but as they were all dressed alike in khaki, this was made a ground for interference, and the officer proceeded to cut some buttons off their tunics, and the rank badges off the arms of the sergeant and corporal. I had previously ordered my men to disarm, and they submitted very quietly to this disfigurement of their clothes. My chief offence, however, was the fact that I was flying the Union Jack, which my men carried with them, as they were accustomed to do on all their expeditions. I mildly put the question to the officer as to whether he expected me to fly the Russian flag, or any other except that of my own country, but it seemed that it was a most serious offence for an Englishman to display the flag under which he had been born and for which he had fought, unless he held some position in the official oligarchy of the country.

In the meantime a fearful row was going on amongst my people and the other Kikuyu who lived near Mberri, who had joined them. The officers asked me why I had brought all those men there, saying that there was bound to be a fight, and no end of trouble. I told them that there would be no trouble with my men, as I could manage them all right. They asked me to disarm them, and I agreed to do so, provided that they would be responsible for their weapons, and on their undertaking to do so, I explained to the chiefs that it was the white men's wish that they should disarm. This they very reluctantly consented to do, and gave up their weapons on my assuring them that they would be restored to them.

When my men were all disarmed, and their

weapons had been safely stowed in a tent, under the care of a sentry, the official announced that I was to consider myself a prisoner as well. To this I merely replied, " All right," thinking that if I expressed the annoyance and resentment that I felt it would only lead to more unpleasantness and possible trouble, of which I saw quite enough possibilities already. I was told that I should be allowed to retain my cook and personal servants, and that no restraint would be put upon my movements, provided that I would give my word of honour not to attempt to clear out. As my real offence was that I had brought into a state of order a country which, previous to my coming, had such a reputation that no official would set foot across the border if he could help it, I had no cause to fear the results of an investigation into my conduct, and I made up my mind to await calmly the termination of this comedy. Besides, I thought that my personal influence might very likely be needed to prevent some " regrettable occurrence." Both the officials were uncertain as to what the natives might do and any hasty or foolish act might easily have set the whole country in a blaze. So I retired to my tent and amused myself for a great part of the day with a gramophone which I had brought with me. Of course, my men could not understand what had happened, and, fortunately, none of them knew that I was under arrest.

In the meantime my men were being questioned as to what had happened in the Kikuyu country during the time that I had been there, and the following day an askari came to my tent and presented me with a lengthy document, written on blue paper, which proved to be a summons to appear that day before the officers in charge of the fort. The summons read something after the following style : " I charge you, John Boyes, that during your residence in the Kenia district you waged war, set shauris, personated Government, went on six punitive expeditions, and committed dacoity." I must confess that I read over this formidable list of charges with some amusement, though I was well aware that any one of them, if proved, meant capital punishment. There was one item on the list that I could not make out, and I took the first opportunity of inquiring the meaning of the word " dacoity," which was a term I had never heard used in the country before. I remembered reading a book called " The Last of the Dacoits," and it struck me that either the title of the book was wrong, or that the official, in his anxiety to fulfil his instructions to pile up as heavy a list of crimes against me as possible, had allowed his imagination to run away with him. It was explained to me that " Dacoit " was an Indian term, meaning a native outlaw.

At the time appointed I presented myself at the " court-house," which was a primitively constructed mud-hut, furnished with two chairs and a table, and as the two former were occupied by the officers, there was nothing left for me but to make myself as comfortable as possible on the corner of the table, which I did, much to the scandal of the two officials. The charge having been read over to me, I was cautioned in the same manner that an English bobby cautions a prisoner, that anything I might say, &c., and then I was asked what I had to say. I told them that I certainly had nothing to say to them one way, or the other, and would reserve my defence, and the proceedings—which were of a purely formal character—were then over, and I returned to my tent.

The next four days were spent in collecting evidence against me, and as nobody could be persuaded to go to my headquarters to collect evidence against me on the spot, the soldier finally went, taking with him the whole of his troops, while during his absence the civilian gathered all the information

he could from the chiefs and other natives at
Mberri.

When they had, as they thought, obtained sufficient
evidence to secure my conviction, the Kikuyu who had
come in with me had their arms restored to them, and
I and my personal bodyguard, together with about
two hundred native witnesses, were sent down to
Nairobi under charge of an escort of about ten native
soldiers, commanded by a black sergeant! The situation was ludicrously Gilbertian. Here was I, a (so-
called) dangerous outlaw, being sent down to be
tried for my life on a series of awful indictments,
through a country in which I had only to lift a finger
to call an army of savage warriors to my assistance.
I was accompanied by a personal following twenty
times as numerous as the guard of ten natives who
kept me prisoner, and who trembled every time they
passed a native village lest the inhabitants should
rush out and wipe them out of existence; while on
the first day out the humour of the situation was
considerably increased by the sergeant in charge of
the escort handing me the large blue envelope containing the statement of the evidence against me, with
a request that I would take charge of it for him, as
he was afraid he might lose it! I must say
that I thoroughly appreciated the humour of the
whole affair. I was the only mounted man in the
whole outfit, still having my mule, and it struck
me as distinctly amusing that I should be practically
taking myself down to Nairobi, to be tried for
my life, with the whole of the evidence under my
arm!

During the journey, which, though only sixty miles
in a straight line, took us five days, as we had to
pick a path—there being then no road—and to avoid
several swamps, some of the soldiers tried to make
my men carry their loads; but I thought that this
was going a little too far, and would not allow
anything of the sort. We saw plenty of game

along the road, and also some lions, but as I was, of course, without my rifle, I could not do any shooting.

When we arrived at Nairobi I presented myself at the Government headquarters, which were then in a little tin shanty, now used by some Indian coolies as a wash-house, while the remainder of the party sat down outside whilst I went in to see the official. The Goanese clerk who inquired my business told me that the Sub-Commissioner was very busy just then and I could not see him. It was quite remarkable how very busy these officials always were when any one, not of the official or missionary class, wanted to see them. I had always experienced the same difficulty in getting an interview, and no doubt the clerk thought that I had come to make one of my usual complaints. On this occasion I did not happen to be in a hurry, so telling the clerk that I would call back in about an hour's time, I went for a stroll round the town, and took the opportunity of having a look at Nairobi. On my return I was received by the Sub-Commissioner, who asked me what I wanted, so I handed him the packet containing the statement of evidence, and when he had looked through it he said that he would make arrangements at once to have me sent down to Mombasa.

Things were done in a different way here, and I quickly realised the change when I got outside the office and found myself surrounded by a guard of six Indian soldiers with fixed bayonets.

That same day I was taken by the afternoon train to Mombasa, under charge of the escort of Indian soldiers, with a white officer in command, and on arriving there I was handed over to another white official. After some considerable delay, the papers apparently not being in order in some respect, I was duly admitted to the Mombasa jail, which was the old Portuguese fort—a massive building, whose

frowning walls rise sheer above the cliff command-
ing the entrance to Mombasa. Many a time, in
days gone by, has the tide of battle rolled around
these grim walls, the many sanguinary conflicts in
which it has figured having earned for Mombasa the
title of the " Isle of War." Looked at from the
outside, the fort is a gloomy-looking place, with its
huge entrance gates guarded by sentries; but its
extent is best judged from the inside, and I found
that there was plenty of room within its massive
walls; while the apartment allotted to my use proved
to be much more comfortable than I had expected—
being, in fact, quite on a par with, if it did not sur-
pass, the accommodation which the only hotel in
Mombasa at that time could provide. I found that
I was perfectly free to roam about the fort at will,
though, of course, I was not allowed to pass outside
the gates.

I had been incarcerated in the fort for some weeks
before any of my friends got to know of my arrest,
and then one of them, Mr Claude Smith, also a
trader and hunter, like myself, hearing of my position, came down to Mombasa to see me. After having paid me a visit, he got the only lawyer in the
country, who was a Parsee, to conduct my defence;
while a few days later these two managed to secure
my release, on a bail of 10,000 rupees, and I left the
fort and went up to Nairobi.

The bare statement that Claude Smith came down
to Mombasa to see me, and secured my release on
10,000 rupees bail, will probably not convey the idea
to the general reader that he did anything calling
for special notice. But, when the facts of the case
are taken into consideration, it will be seen that the
comradeship which existed among us early pioneers
in that wild, official-ridden territory, was of a kind
which does not usually flourish among the stay-at-
home, arm-chair critics who, from the comfort of the
club fireside or the smug atmosphere of the Exeter

Hall platform, condemn the traders and settlers as irredeemable blackguards or, as one complacent official described them to a gathering of uneducated natives, as *washenzi Uliya*, the translation of which is " the savages of Europe." In the first place, although I had no claim on him whatever, he came down some four hundred miles from Naivasha, where he was hunting, leaving his expedition for the purpose, and found the 10,000 rupees bail—which had to be actually deposited—from his own pocket, and remained with me until the case was dismissed— thus sacrificing many weeks of valuable time in my interests. Further than all this, he incurred the bitter enmity of the official who had instigated the whole business against me, and who never rested until he had fabricated a similar charge against my friend, needless to say with the result of triumphal acquittal for both of us.

When my trial came on, I found that all the charges against me, except the one of dacoity, had been withdrawn; which fact only served to confirm the information I had received—were any confirmation needed—as to the origin of, and reason for, the whole conspiracy against me. The trial was by judge and jury, and after hearing the evidence against me the court acquitted me, and I left the court-house, as the judge said, without a stain on my character—the judge even going so far as to say that he did not understand why the case had been brought at all, and, finally, apologising to me for the waste of my valuable time !

As to why the case had been brought I could have given the judge a good deal of information which would have enlightened him considerably, but as I had come so triumphantly out of the matter, I did not see that I had anything to gain by stirring up the mud. At that time there were not more than a dozen independent white men in the country; all the rest were Government officials, missionaries, or

men engaged in the construction of the Uganda
Railway, and, for some reason or other, the govern-
ing class were always bitterly hostile to the commercial and hunting element, and took every occasion of impressing upon us that we were not wanted
in the country. Further than this, some men holding
the Government appointments at that time were by
no means representative of the best elements of
officialdom.[1] This state of affairs is by no means
peculiar to British East Africa, but has been experienced in most of our other African Crown Colonies,
and, indeed, prevailed in many of them up to quite
recently, and may do so yet for all I know. Fortunately, so far as British East Africa is concerned,
there are now good prospects of the carrying out
of a saner and more intelligent policy under the
guidance of the new Governor, Sir Percy
Girouard. If the colony is ever to become anything
more than a happy hunting ground for official
inefficients, every assistance must be given to those
who are willing to invest their money in the
country, and petty officialism must be put in
its proper place in the machinery of government.

In my case there were many mixed motives under-
lying the conspiracy to get me ousted from the
Kikuyu country, and if possible from the dependency,
but it is perhaps better that I should be silent about
all this. One reason, perhaps, for desiring my removal was the apprehension that existed out there
that the authorities at home might think that after
all the man who single-handed had reduced to peace
and order a country into which no white man had
ever successfully entered before, might not be a bad
one to entrust with its future administration in the
interests of the Empire. Of course, such an intru-

[1] It must be remembered that the administration of
the country was just starting. The Government had
to put up with what officials they could get.

sion into the sacred official class by a common trader,
who actually understood the natives—as far as a
white man may—and was able to exercise a kindly
influence over them, was to be prevented at all
hazards, even at the cost of the said trader's life if
need be.

For my part, although no man likes to give up
practically supreme power, even among savages, I
had always recognized that the day must come—
and had been at some trouble to prepare the natives
for it—when the administration of the country would
be duly taken over by the official bureaucracy, and
my only aim was to assist the officials as far as possible. Unfortunately, the petty spite and official
arrogance and inefficiency of certain individuals
defeated my object, and within a comparatively short
period I was grieved to find that my old friend and
blood brother, Wagombi, irritated at the tactless way
in which he was treated by the new officials, was
carrying fire and sword through the whole country,
and raiding almost up to the walls of the boma
where the new Administrator lay trembling and
afraid to venture a quarter of a mile outside his own
camp.

However, as I have already said, all those who
have the true interests of British East Africa at heart
are hoping for a better state of things under the
experienced and enlightened administration of Sir
Percy Girouard.

After the fiasco of my trial, I returned to Karuri's,
and continued my food-buying, taking the supplies
into Naivasha as before. I still experienced the same
trouble with the Kalyera natives on the way down
with the food for the Government stations, and finally
the matter was reported to the Governor, Sir Charles
Eliot, who resided at Zanzibar, which was then the
headquarters of the Government. As a result of
these representations, an expedition was sent out
under Captain Wake, of the East African Rifles,

with Mr McLellan as civil officer, and I was asked
to accompany them as guide and intelligence
officer. I was only too pleased to have this
opportunity of proving to the Government my
readiness to help, and I willingly agreed to go with
the expedition.

CHAPTER XI

Origin of the Kikuyu—The family—Circumcision—
Marriage—Land tenure—Missionaries

IT may be of interest to the general reader if I
give, in a single chapter, a brief account of the
manners and customs of the Kikuyu people, and
some description of the country in which they live.
It must be borne in mind that the information contained in this section is not the result of direct ques-
tioning of the people, as it is well known to all who
have any *real* knowledge of the African native that
to ask directly for information of this sort from him
simply results in the acquisition of a large amount
of information which, however interesting it may be
to read, contains the smallest possible proportion of
actual truth. Therefore, the account of the Kikuyu
and their country given in the following pages is
the result of my own personal knowledge and observation during the period of my residence among
them. It may not be as picturesque as some other
published accounts, but I am prepared to vouch for
its accuracy.

Owing to the fact that no accurate map of this
part of Africa has yet been prepared, it is a matter of
some difficulty to give exactly the boundaries and
dimensions of the Kikuyu country; but, roughly
speaking, it is bounded on the north by a line which
almost coincides with the Equator; on the west by
the Aberdare Range, a range of bamboo-covered hills,
uninhabited by any tribe; on the south by a kind of
debatable land, forming part of the Athi Plain,

extending from Nairobi to Fort Hall, to the south of which lies the Wakamba country; on the east, for a considerable distance by the Tana River, beyond which it only extends for a short distance towards the north-east. These boundaries may have been somewhat modified since the opening up of the country by the Government of British East Africa, but in the main they are still correct. The area of this district would be about four thousand square miles.

As I never attempted to take any sort of census during my " reign," I can only give approximately the population, but I should say, as far as I was able to ascertain, that the total number of the tribe would be about half a million—rather more than less —of whom the women outnumbered the men considerably, the constant warfare tending to keep the number of the male population at a fairly steady figure.

The accounts given of the origin of the Kikuyu tribe vary considerably, and the nigger's talent for fiction, and his readiness to oblige any one—particularly a white man—who asks for a legend, make it extremely difficult to distinguish where truth ends and fiction begins; but I will give the two principal accounts as they were given to me, and my own opinion of the credibility of both, and let the reader judge for himself.

The first story is that given me by Karuri, the chief who was my first friend among these interesting people, who was certainly one of the most intelligent natives I have ever come in contact with. His account was that the original inhabitants of the country, a tribe called the Asi, were hunters who took no interest in agriculture, and that the Kikuyu were a tribe who came into the country, and purchased tracts of land from the Asi for purposes of cultivation. Gradually more and more of the Kikuyu came in until they had cleared most of the forest

land of which the country originally consisted, while
the Asi were gradually absorbed into the Kikuyu
tribe by marriage, or wandered farther afield in
search of the game which the increasing population
and the clearing of the forests had driven away to
new retreats. Karuri himself based his strongest
claim to his chieftaincy on the fact that he was a
direct descendant of these Asi.

The other account, which was given me by a
headman named Kasu, now a powerful chief under
the new regime, reminds one somewhat of the story
of Ishmael. The legend runs that a Masai warrior,
living on the borders of what is now the Kikuyu
country, but was then a vast forest, inhabited by a
race of dwarfs, of whom the Kikuyu speak as the
Maswatch-wanya, was in the habit of ill-treating one
of his wives to such an extent that she used from
time to time to take refuge among the dwarfs,
returning to her husband's kraal after each flight.
Finally his treatment became so bad that she fled to
the dwarfs and remained there, giving birth to a son
shortly after her definite settlement among them.
Later on, the story runs, she had children to her
own son, which children intermarried with the Maswatch-wanya, and from their offspring the present
Kikuyu race derive their descent.

Of the two accounts, my observation would lead
me to look for the truth rather in the direction of
the latter than the former. In the first place, as I
think I have before pointed out, a strong physical
resemblance exists between the Kikuyu and the
Masai; the former, indeed, might almost be taken
for a shorter, more stockily built branch of the latter
race, while I could easily pick out a hundred
Kikuyu who, mixed with an equal number of Masai,
could not be told from the latter, even by an expert.
Again, the weapons and war-dress of the two races
are identical—a fact which to any one who is aware
of the unique character of the Masai weapons is a

strong point in itself. Further, when actually on the war-path—and *only* then—the Kikuyu are in the habit of singing a Masai war-song, in the Masai tongue, referring to a former noted warrior chief of the Masai named Bartion. Again, their manner of circumcising the young men is exactly the same as that practised by the Masai, which differs from the custom of any other race, as I shall show later on. The name for God, Ngai, is the same in both peoples, and they both have a similar custom of retiring to a so-called " sacred grove " in the bush, where they slaughter a sheep, which is afterwards roasted and eaten in honour of their god.

These points, to my mind, all go to show a connexion between the Kikuyu and the Masai, rather than, as some inquirers argue, between the Kikuyu and the Wakamba. Of course, in the districts bordering on the Wakamba country, where it has been customary for the two tribes to seize one another's women in their frequent raids, many of the Kikuyu show traces of Wakamba blood, while on the Masai border the traces of Masai influence are stronger than in the districts more remote; but I am not arguing on the basis of the border districts, but from the race as a whole. Again, the Wakamba, though not now known to be cannibals, still follow the practice prevalent among cannibal tribes of filing the teeth to a sharp point—a practice unknown both to the Masai and the Kikuyu. The Wakamba also are eaters of raw meat, while the Masai, though blood-drinkers, always cook their meat, and the Kikuyu are practically vegetarians. In the manner of dressing the hair, too, the Kikuyu follow the Masai fashion of plaiting strands of bark fibre into the hair, which is then done up in a sort of pigtail, while the Wakamba wear the covering provided by Nature without any fancy additions.

Another custom common to both the Masai and Kikuyu, though not practised by the Wakamba, is

that of wearing the most extraordinary ear ornaments, which, as mentioned earlier in the book, are
sometimes as large as a condensed milk tin, and are
worn passed through holes specially made in the
lobe of the ear. The practice is to pierce the lobe
of the boys' ears some time in early childhood, and
from that time onwards the aperture then made is
gradually enlarged by the wearing of a succession of
wooden plugs or discs of graduated sizes, until an
object as large as a large-sized condensed milk tin
can be easily passed through it. This operation
extends over some years, and the natural result is to
convert the ring of flesh into what looks like—and
as far as feeling is concerned, might as well be—a
leather loop, which sometimes hangs down far
enough to touch the shoulder. It is the great ambition of every Kikuyu youth to be able to wear a
bigger ear ornament than his neighbour, and, in
order to attain the desired end, I have known them
to pass a straight stick of wood through the hole
in the lobe of one ear, across the back of the neck,
through the lobe of the other, thus keeping them
both constantly stretched.

The country itself is very rough, and it is often a
matter of difficulty to find a level piece sufficiently
large to pitch one's camp on. It is situated at an
elevation of some six thousand feet above sea-level,
and consists of a series of ranges of low hills,
divided by deep valleys, through most of which flows
a stream of greater or less magnitude, none of
which ever seem to become quite dried up, even in
the driest of dry seasons. On account of the comparatively temperate climate, due to the elevation,
and of the extreme fertility of the soil, the country
is an ideal spot for the native agriculturist, who
gets his two crops a year with a minimum of labour.
Consequently the country is very thickly populated;
in fact, I do not know any part where, on raising
the tribal war-cry, I could not, in an extremely short

space of time, gather at least a couple of thousand fighting men. The principal crops are the sweet potato, *kigwa* (a kind of yam of very large dimensions), and *ndoma* (a vegetable something after the fashion of a turnip, with leaves from three to four feet long and about eighteen inches wide at their widest part). Bananas are the only fruit that I ever came across, but they grow large quantities of sugar-cane, beans of various kinds (from my fondness for which in preference to sweet potatoes I got my native name of Karanjai, or " The eater of beans "), and another vegetable, which seemed to be a cross between a bean and a pea and which grew on a bush; of grains they have several, of which the principal are maize, *matama*, which is the same as the Indian dhurra and is found all over Africa, *umkanori*, which resembles canary-seed in appearance, and *mawhali*, a somewhat similar seed to the umkanori, from which the fermented gruel known as ujuru is made. The Kikuyu seem to be possessed of a perfect mania for cultivation, their practice being to work a plot of ground until it begins to show signs of exhaustion, when it is allowed to lie fallow or used only for grazing stock for a period of seven years, new ground being broken to take its place in the meanwhile. All the Kikuyu keep stock of some kind, either sheep, cattle, or goats—sometimes all three—which are principally used as currency for the purpose of paying fines and buying wives, the quantity of meat eaten being very small.

The system of government is somewhat peculiar, but appeared to be a form of the feudal system, based on the family. A village generally consists of members of one family, the headman being the father, who had originally settled in that particular spot with his wives. Each wife has her own hut, her own *shamba*, or allotment for cultivation, and her own store-house, in which the proceeds of her labour are kept. Each woman lives in her own hut, with her family round her, until the boys are old enough to marry, when they set up their own hut, or huts, according to the number of wives in which they are wealthy enough to indulge. The headman or patriarch of the family, in my time, ruled the village, and, within bounds, had the right of punishing any breach of discipline—even to the extent of killing a disobedient son and burning his huts. The women are well treated, and, as they perform all the work of the family, with the exception of clearing new ground for cultivation, prefer to marry a man with two or three other wives rather than a bachelor, as the work of keeping their lord and master in comfort is thus rendered lighter.

Marriage is, as in most savage tribes, by purchase, the usual purchase price of a woman being thirty sheep. There is no marriage ceremony in vogue among them, but after the handing over of the girl by her father in exchange for the sheep a feast is usually held to celebrate the event. Occasionally the husband is allowed to make the payments on the instalment plan, but this is not encouraged, as it is apt to lead to quarrelling and disagreements. The youthful marriages common among such tribes do not prevail among the Kikuyu, as no man is allowed to marry until he has been circumcised, which operation usually takes place about the age of seventeen or eighteen, and he does not generally take a wife until two or three years later; while the usual age for marriage among the women is eighteen, though the operation which corresponds to circumcision in their case is performed as soon as they reach the age of puberty.

This practice of circumcision of the males at such a late age appears to prevail only among the Masai and Kikuyu, all other African races, so far as I can learn, following the Jewish custom and performing the operation during infancy. The method of performing the operation in vogue with these two tribes

also differs from that in use elsewhere, so that a
description of it may be of interest. On the day
fixed for the ceremony the boys all turn out some
time before daylight and are taken down to the
river, where they have to stand for half an hour up
to the waist in the ice-cold water until they are
absolutely numb with the cold. They are then taken
out and led to the operator, who nearly severs the
foreskin with two cuts of his knife, then, folding
the severed portion back, secures it on the under
side with a thorn driven through the flesh. The
boy then returns to his village and rests for a few
days until the wound is healed. No boy is supposed
to utter a sound during the operation, and it is
probable that the numbing effect of the icy bath
prevents their feeling any or very much pain. In
the case of the girls also the bath in the cold river
is a preliminary to the operation, and neither boys
nor girls ever seem to suffer any serious consequences
from this rough-and-ready operation. In the case of
the girls the operation, which consists of the excision
of the clitoris, is performed by an old woman, whose
special duty it is to perform the operation with one
of the razors used for shaving the head.

The various sections of the tribe are ruled by
chiefs, of whom the principal during my stay in the
country were Wagombi, Karkerrie, and Karuri, but
in addition to these there were innumerable petty
chieftains, many of whom owed no allegiance to any
higher authority in the country. Kingship, or chief-
ship, seemed to be decided mainly on the principle
that might is right, though it was of great advantage for a candidate for the headship of any section
of the tribe to have a reputation for magic—or medicine, as they call it. Wealth and intelligence also
counted for something, and a chief who had proved
himself a brave warrior and good administrator
would generally be allowed to retain his headship of
a district so long as he lived, though it did not

follow that his son would succeed to his honours unless he were capable of taking hold of the reins of government with a firm hand. In spite of the apparent uncertainty of succession, there is seldom any trouble with regard to it, as it is generally pretty well known some time before a vacancy takes place who the next chief will be, although I never found that there was any sort of election to the office.

The chief, once accepted, is autocratic in the ordinary details of government, trying all cases himself and pronouncing sentence, from which there is no appeal; but in matters of moment affecting the general welfare of the people he is aided in coming to a decision by the counsels of the assembled elders of his district, a body something after the fashion of the old Saxon Witan.

For ordinary infractions of the law, or offences against his authority as chief, he pronounced such punishment as his discretion and judgment dictated; but for cases of wounding or murder a regular scale of fines was laid down—fining being the usual punishment, except in cases of open rebellion. Open rebellion generally entailed a descent on the offenders by the chief's warriors, and the wiping out of the rebellious villages and their inhabitants. For an ordinary case of wounding the fine was ten sheep, while for the murder of a woman it was thirty sheep —the price which her husband would have had to pay for her on marriage—and for a man a hundred sheep. The tenure of land is very simple, the freehold being vested in the man who takes the trouble to make the clearing, and as there is plenty of space for all, and the wants of the people are few, anything in the shape of agrarian agitation is unknown; in fact. during the whole of my stay in the country I never knew any instance of a dispute over land.

It must be borne in mind that many great changes have taken place in the Kikuyu country, and in British East Africa generally, since the period, some

ten years since, covered by this book. In the days
when I started on my first contract for the convey-
ance of food to the troops engaged in the suppression
of the Soudanese mutiny, the spot on which Nairobi,
the present capital of the colony stands, was simply
a patch of swampy ground on the edge of the plain
which extends to the borders of the hilly Kikuyu
country. Here the railway construction people
pitched one of their settlements and put up a station,
and from this has risen the town of some fifteen
thousand inhabitants, of whom fully one thousand
are white, a larger proportion than can be found in
any settlement of the same age on the continent of
Africa, while I may add that everything points to an
increased rather than a diminished rate of progres-
sion !

Nairobi is no bush settlement, where one expects
to " rough it " as part of the ordinary daily routine.
On leaving the train one can engage a cab, or even
a motor, to drive one to a good hotel; if you know
any one in the town, you can be put up for an
excellent club; while one's commercial requirements
are met by a fine post-office, banks of good standing,
and stores where one may obtain anything that the
most fastidious European or savage tastes can
require.

Undoubtedly the colony of British East Africa has
everything in its favour and, given ordinary luck,
has a great future before it. The climate is everything that the European settler could desire. Being
about six thousand feet above sea-level, the country
is not subjected to the extremes of heat and wet which
prevail in other parts of the continent, but has
merely a good average rainfull, while the temperature seldom exceeds 75° in the shade, even in the
hottest weather. The soil, particularly in the
Kikuyu district, is extremely fertile, and will grow
almost any European vegetable, and most European
fruits, in addition to wheat, coffee, cocoa, tea, sugar,

and tobacco, as well as cotton, rubber, sisal hemp, sansovera fibre, and, of course, on the coast, the ubiquitous cocoanut. On the whole, British East Africa presents as good an opportunity to the man of limited capital, with a capacity for work, as any spot to be found in the length and breadth of the British Empire. In addition to agriculture, such industries as cattle-farming, sheep-farming, pig-breeding, and ostrich-farming are already being carried on with great success. Under the wise administration of the present Governor, Sir Percy Girouard, the prospects of the country are improving by leaps and bounds. This is principally due to two important factors : the encouragement given by the Governor to capitalists willing to invest money in the colony; and his full and frank recognition, for the first time in the history of the colony, that the future of this valuable dependency lies in the hands of the settlers, rather than in those of the official caste.

The value of land is rapidly increasing, and estates which, ten years ago, could have been bought for 2s. 8d. an acre are now fetching 20s. an acre, though grants may still be obtained from the Government land office.

In the Kikuyu country itself vast changes have, of course, taken place in the ten years which have elapsed since I was supreme there. Four or five Government stations have been established, roads have been opened up in various directions, while many white settlers have come in, and are doing well, in addition to the swarm of missionaries of various sects who have settled all over the country; in fact, I gave my own house to one of the first, I think I may say the first—a Roman Catholic priest —who came into the country. The people themselves have settled down quietly under the new conditions, and pay the hut-tax regularly, which is a by no means inconsiderable item in the annual revenue of the colony. The Kikuyu are excellent workers,

and are now to be met with in every part of the
dependency, and in almost every trade, while the
chiefs have taken to building stone houses in place
of their native huts, and riding mules. In my
opinion the Kikuyu will ultimately become the most
important among the native races of this part of
the continent, owing to their greater intelligence,
industry, and adaptability.

Of course, at the present day, my name is little
more than a legend among the Kikuyu, around
which many wonderful stories have been built up
by the people. In the nine years which have elapsed
since I left the country many of the older men who
knew me have died, while the rising generation
who, as children, only knew of me as the most
powerful influence in the province, have only vague
memories of actual happenings, which they have
gradually embroidered until I should have great
difficulty in recognizing some of the occurrences myself in their present form.

A book of this sort will probably be looked upon
as incomplete without some expression of opinion as
to the value of missions and the missionary influence.
It must not be inferred from the various remarks
scattered through the book that I am one of that
fairly numerous body who, with considerable experience to back their opinion, profess to regard the
missionary as the worst curse that can fall on a
newly-opened country, but I do say that the whole
system on which these missions are conducted re-
quires to be thoroughly revised. The primary mistake, from which most of the trouble springs, is the
assumption, to which all missionaries seem to be
officially compelled to subscribe, that the African
negro is, or can be made by education, the moral
and intellectual equal of the white man, and that
by teaching him to read and write and say the
Lord's Prayer by rote the inherent characteristics
resulting from centuries of savagery can be utterly

nullified in the course of a year or two. The delib-
erate and considered opinion of those best qualified
to know, the men who have to live among these
people, not for a year or two, but for a lifetime,
brought into constant and more really intimate contact with them than the great majority of missionaries, is, that education in the narrow meaning of
the term is a very doubtful blessing to the average
negro compared with the enormous benefits to be
conferred by a sound course of industrial training.
As an instance in point, let us take the case of
Uganda, where the missionary has had a free hand,
such as he has probably had in no other part of the
world, for the last twenty years. Yet, after all this
time, there is hardly a single Uganda artisan to be
found—and those of poor quality—in Uganda itself;
British East Africa has to look to the native of
India to find the skilled artisans required for the
service of the community. And it must be borne in
mind that the Waganda are undoubtedly the most
intelligent of all the native races of East Africa, so
that the settler may fairly consider himself justified
when he charges the missionaries with neglecting,
practically entirely, one of the greatest aids to the
civilization of the native that he could possibly use.
The native, properly trained to handicrafts, and able
to understand the advantage of skill in his particular
line, would be much more likely, as his means
increased, to see the advantages of civilization, and
to appreciate the benefits of that education which,
as often as not, now lands him in jail; while the
civilized negro, become a really useful member of
the community, would also be much more likely to
prove a satisfactory convert to Christianity than the
material at present paraded as such, of whom the
average white man with experience of Africa will
tell you that he would not have a " mission native "
    a servant at any price.
    Let the missionaries turn their minds and funds to

the industrial, as well as the moral and religious, instruction of the natives, and they will find every settler in the land prepared to support their efforts, while the Empire will, undoubtedly, benefit enormously in every way.

Finally, one of the greatest difficulties which hampers the development of our African colonies, and renders the task of the administrator who really *does* know something of the work he has taken in hand a heart-breaking one, is the utter inability of the good people at home to realize the absolutely irrefutable truth contained in Kipling's statement that " East is East, and West is West, and never the twain shall meet." The average missionary and new-comer to Africa generally arrives with his mind stored with the statements contained in the reports of missionary societies or the books of well-to-do globe-trotters, and is firmly convinced that he knows all there is to be known about the country and its people. When he has been a year or two in the country he will, if he has any remnants of common sense left, begin to realize that it is about time he began to try to learn something of the people among whom his lot is cast; while at the end of ten, fifteen, or more years he will frankly confess the utter impossibility of the white man ever being able to, as an able African administrator once put it, " get inside the negro's skin," and really know him thoroughly. I question if there have ever, in the history of the world, been twenty pure-bred whites altogether who have really known the native of Africa, and if you hear a man boasting that he " knows the nigger thoroughly," you may safely put him down as a man of very limited experience of the negroid races.

The ultimate solution of the negro problem lies, not in the " poor coloured brother " direction, but in training him in handicrafts, and thus making him a useful, productive member of the community; and as soon as this fact is recognized, and carried to its

logical result, so soon will the " colour problem "
—which at present weighs heavily on the mind of
every thinking white man who really realizes what
it means—cease to be the ever-present bogey of our
African Administration.

And here for the moment I will end my story.
It was my intention, when I first started to write
this account of my experiences among the Kikuyu,
to have extended the period of this book to the
times of my more recent adventures on the African
continent. I found, however, that space would not
allow me to include all I wished to put down in
writing in one small volume. I have, I think much
more to relate which might be of interest to the
general reader. I have spent the last ten years of
my life either exploring in the wilds of the Dark
Continent or have been occupied as a professional
hunter of big game, and should this book of mine
find any favour with the public, I hope in a short
time to recommence my labours as an author again.

My next experience immediately after the facts
related in this book was to take the Governor of
British East Africa, Sir Charles Eliot, on a personally
conducted tour to the scenes of my adventures and
throughout the wilder parts of his domain. Later,
many stirring adventures with lion and elephant
have been my lot. My wanderings have led me
across the desert from British East Africa into
Abyssinia, into the Congo territory and elsewhere.
I hope some of the adventures which befell me in
these travels may, in the future, prove interesting to
the public.